About the A

Pastor Ebenezer Abodunde Solawon is
and a teacher by calling. He acquired his knowledge through the
inspiration of God and also attended Obafemi Awolowo University
(UNIFECS), Adekunle Ajasin University Akungba-Akoko, Faith
Christian Theological Seminary (Sango-Ota, Ogun State, Nigeria) in
Conjunction with Central Christian University (USA), International
Institute of Chaplaincy (Ota, Nigeria) and Olabisi Onabanjo
University, Ogun State, Nigeria where he studied Law, Theology and
Chaplaincy, Missiology, etc.

He has been a teacher for more than two decades at different academic
strata - Primary, Secondary and Tertiary Institutions. He is a seasoned
speaker at Churches, Seminars and Conferences.

About the Book

A Natural man thinks of the world as vanity or complete nonsense because he is ignorant of God and God's purpose for him and the entire creation. God did not create the earth and leave it to wander aimlessly, He provided an Ark as a meeting point. The Old testament ark with its fulfillment in Jesus Christ did not only portray the presence of God among men, it also contains the eternal purpose of God for the earth. The ark is the covenant of God and purpose for the people He created. For any man to discover his purpose and fulfill it, he needs the Ark in his or her life. The more you allow the ark to freely control you, the more you are successful in achieving your eternal purpose. Those who live without purpose, have obviously lost contact with the Ark and shall continue to wander all over the earth like Cain who lived under a divine curse. This bible study series is written to reconcile man with God and reconnect man with his own purpose of living through a victorious life and an acceptable worship which is eternally rewarding.

THE ARK IN MORTAL TABERNACLE

(A Bible Study Series One)

Ebenezer Abodunde Solawon

THE ARK IN MORTAL TABERNACLE
(A Bible Study Series One)

Publisher: Amz Marketing Hub

Writer: Pastor Ebenezer Abodunde Solawon

E-mail: Pastorsea2005@yahoo.com

For further enquiries, please contact:

Ebenezer Abodunde Solawon –

GSM: +447570640219 (UK), +2348064582682 (Nigeria).

(Pounds Account) Bank of Scotland – 12274764 – Sort Code: 804511), (Naira Account) Polaris Bank - Ikorodu – 1012985470.

Unless otherwise indicated, all scripture quotations are taken from the New International Version, King James Version and the New King James Version of the Bible.

Dedication

I dedicate this book to God who inspired the writing; my family and to all who found the book highly invaluable.

Acknowledgements

I am grateful to God for teaching me His Word and counting me among the great company of those who publish it. I am grateful to my family for their support and to all people who shall study and teach from this book.

Thank you all!

Foreword

The admonition of Apostle Paul to us in 11 Timothy 2:15 is to study to show ourselves approved unto God, a glorious workman who need not be ashamed but who will rightly divide the word of truth.

The need to heed this admonition becomes very pronounced when it is realised, using the words of John Dryden (the great 17th-century Poet): "Errors, like straws, upon the surface flow", He who would search for pearls must dive below. The believer who is not ready to make an in-depth search of the scriptures like the noble Berean Christians (of Acts 17:10 & 11) runs the risk of easily getting entangled with false doctrines which are all over the place and being dangled like carrots by false teachers who keep multiplying by the day. This, of course, is one of the key signs of the end time (1 John 4:1), which our Lord Jesus Christ warned us to beware of in Mathews 7:15, 24::24 & 25 and Mark 13, 22 & 23. It is in light of this that a Bible Study Guide like this is crucial and an excellent aid for inquisitive believers who are hungry and thirsty after righteousness, as well as those earnest enquirers who want to correctly digest the word of God. I am highly impressed with the effort of the young author, who is both a practising missionary and a Pastor.

Undoubtedly, the subject he has delved into is spirit-inspired. The Ark, to the children of Israel, symbolised God's presence. May you begin to experience His ever-abiding presence as you study this material in Jesus' Name. The writer of psalms 139 asserted that none of us could really run away from the presence of God. No matter where we are, we are very much before and within the all-seeing eyes of the omniscient God and creator of heaven and the entire universe. The author had requested that I write this foreword for over three weeks, but I have not been able to pull myself together until this moment when I am on a flight Boeing 737 aeroplane to Abuja. As I write, even in the clouds, according to the pilot, at an altitude of 33,000 feet above sea level, I feel the awesome presence of God.

I commend this study material to you and pray that the Lord will use it to illuminate your spirit-man and take you to a higher level in your walk of faith as you digest and meditate on it.

J. O. ODUPITAN

Area Pastor
Divine Covenant Church Area,
Lagos Province 22, RCCG

THE ARK IN MORTAL TABERNACLE (A Bible Study Series One) is a good Bible Study material, which is not only recommended for an adult but for young ones as well. The beautiful analogy of the Ark in both the Old Testament and New Testament is commendable. No doubt, Jesus Christ is the Ark of God in which the secret of the eternal purpose is hidden. However, the Ark that was known to be the Ark of Joy could suddenly become the Ark of Judgement and of death. This is a warning to all Christians. Churches who want the truth and desire the truth will find this book highly invaluable.

Rev Prof. A. Olalekan Dairo
Department of Religious Studies,
Olabisi Onabanjo University,
Ago-lwoye.

It is great joy and very stimulating and illuminating reading the manuscript of this study book which is intended for every believer and follower of Christ. The subject is fascinating – the Ark - and the trajectory is unique as it traces the Ark in various dimensions throughout the Bible: Old and New Testaments; across the lives of notable people of God; its true meanings and application for all believers. The encounters of Noah, Saul, David, the philistines, and Uzzah with the Ark, are some of the stories examined in some detail and practical revelations are put forward for the reader and student to examine. You get the sense that the book put forward the Ark as a pattern of eternal implications and constant applications for all believers.

The author - Pastor Ebenezer, I know so well as a lover of God. I am also blessed to do kingdom work with him. The study guide approach (rather than novel or doctrinal format) adopted by the author in this book, works excellently well as it invites the readers to examine for themselves the principles and truths and then to apply them to practical everyday walk of faith. I strongly commend this book to all believers, seekers, and leaders, as a vital tool in the journey into discipleship and Christian maturity.

Dr Mark Osa Igiehon
City of God, Aberdeen-Scotland

Introduction

A few years back, I led a group out for evangelism. We had preached to the unbelievers the good message of our Lord Jesus Christ and had a free-flow conversation. We thought it would continue like that until we met a group of believers who sat down discussing among themselves. Since the bible taught us to preach in season and out of season, we felt impelled to share the gospel with them too. (2 Timothy 4:2). The following ensued:

"Good Afternoon Sirs and Mas", we greeted to call their attention. "Yes, yes, what do you want?" One of them asked aggressively. "All right Sir, we are here to share with you the gospel of our Lord Jesus Christ," we replied. "My friend, go away! Can't you see we are talking? Go away, I say, or do you want me to slap you?" the man said angrily. "We are sorry for interrupting your discussion," we replied and were set to go. "By the way, you are from which Church?" The man asked curiously. "End time Sir." "No wonder, one of the 419 (fraudulent) churches". I am a Redeemite. I attend Redeemed Church, Redeemed!" He resounded.

When he was neither going to listen nor allow others pay attention, we left in disappointment. The disappointment was not because he did not listen but because he was ready to slap us for preaching Jesus at that moment, even though he is a Christian believer, so to speak.

In the same appalling condition was the case of Ananias and Sapphira. They were counted among the believers and shared continually with the Apostles; still, they were discovered to have been practising Christianity as a religion and not as a life.

Christianity is a life of Christ which must be born in any Born Again believer. It is not a religion or a matter of routine. It is a life lived in accordance with the Kingdom rules. No one is a Christian except when Christ's life is born and grown in his own spirit-man. Like a cobra dies for her children to live, so also must a Christian die for another life to take up his body. The death of your own life is important because "the soul that sinneth shall die" (Ezekiel. 18:4, 20(KJV)) for Christ's life to continue in you.

It is life for life. Christianity is a matter of life and death. That is why it must not be practised as a religion. Now, the dead do not respond again to the living. You are dead, and the life you now live does not belong to you but Christ's. That is why you must take instructions and look up to Jesus Christ for everything else, you will become like Ananias and Sapphira, who, after conversion and open renunciation of former ways of life, still kept on with lies, greediness and love of pleasure rather than the things of God.

They shared with others who sold their possessions and laid everything at the apostles' feet, but when it was their own turn, they kept part of the money and brought the other part to the apostles in the pretence that all was brought. Consequently, the Holy Spirit intervened and removed the "chaff from the wheat" by striking them down because that was not what the Church should be known with. (Acts 5:1-11).

Many people today answer to Christian names, attend church programmes, and choose Christianity when asked to indicate their religion; Pastors, and even church workers alike. They can fight or kill whoever dares to oppose Christianity. Yet, they are "like whitewashed tombs which indeed appear beautiful outwardly, but inside are full of dead men's bones and all uncleanliness" (Matthew 23:27). They draw near Christ with their lips, but their thoughts, speeches, and actions show what is contrary to the faith they profess. (Isaiah 29:13).

We are not Christians just by our names or claims. Instead, we are Christians by what others see us do, which is different from what is prevalent in the world (Acts 11:26). Before anyone can be called a Christian in its real meaning, it must be determined by the position of the Ark in his/her life; how appropriately he worships God and how much he makes himself a companion of the Holy Spirit to live a holy life.

I encourage you, if you are fortunate to get a copy of this book to use it for your private or Church bible study or Sunday school, as the book was led by the Holy Spirit to guide people to have a solid relationship with our Maker. Stay blessed as you get closer to the study proper!

Table of Contents

Study One

THE ARK (PART 1)

MEMORY VERSE: *"And the Israelites enquired of the LORD (In those days the Ark of the Covenant of God was there...)"* (Judge 20:27).

BIBLE PASSAGE: Revelation 11:19, 2 Corinth. 6:16

INTRODUCTION

Have you ever wondered whether or not God treated people differently? Have you ever wondered why some people demonstrate God's power better than others? Has it ever flickered across your mind why God would allow some people more time to repent than others before He washes His hands off them? Have you asked yourself why some people know the truth about God and continue sinning and, in a short period of time, lose their salvation? Yet, others know the truth and sin for years, even decades, and then find God's forgiveness? Have you wondered why God would ask a nation in the Bible to rise and completely wipe out another nation, and yet, He created them all? Why would some people die in their prime age and some beg for death at a stricken old age? Is God partial in His dealings with the people He created? Not at all. In fact, God's word is very clear in telling us that all men are created equal, and every single person can be a child of God, receiving the full inheritance of heaven. The Greek word that is translated impartially is "aprosopolemptos". The word is often used with reference to God's judgement before which there is no respect for persons (Ephesians 6:9, Colossians 3:25). He is not influenced by our physical appearance, skills, or success in life. A great example that demonstrates God is impartial is found in James 2:1-7 where we are warned not to be biased or partial toward people.

That, notwithstanding, as it is written in the book, "Animal Farm", by the famous writer George Orwell:

"All animals are equal, but some animals are more equal than the others," the theology of God's impartiality shows that He treated

1

humans differently despite impartiality being His attribute. The fact of this is that God treasures, protects, and relates with men based on the weight or quantum of their divine assignments; the position of the Ark and the space it occupies in their life. The wider the space, the bigger the Ark. Otherwise, the level of your humility before God and the extent to which you prepare your mind for Christ will determine how awesome the presence of God will manifest in your life. Once you have Christ in you, you have the Ark in you.

Outlines:

1. What is an Ark?
2. Ark as a Symbol
3. The Ark in the Old Testament

What is an Ark?

An Ark is a chest or coffer to keep things sure or secret (Exodus 2:3). An Ark is the great vessel in which Noah and his family were preserved during the flood, (Genesis 6:14, 15, Hebrews 11:7). It is a chest wherein the two tablets of the law (Exodus 25:21, Deuteronomy 10:2), Aaron's rod (Numbers 17:10) and the pot of manna were kept (Exodus 16:33, Hebrews 9:4).

Ark as a Symbol

An Ark is not just a wooden boat built to save Noah and his family. It is a chest which originally existed in Heaven and contains the secrets of the eternal purpose of God (Revelation 11:19). It was at first given to man in a wood form to represent the presence and the characters of God among humankind (Genesis 6:14-22, Exodus 25, 10-22, Joshua. 4:1-11, 6:12-14, 1 Samuel 3:34, 2 Chronicles 5:2-14). It is a place where God and man meet for fellowship (Exodus 25:22). The Ark symbolizes Jesus Christ, the "Emmanuel" who is to live with us as God's presence among men (Isaiah 7:14, Matthew 1:23).

The Ark in the Old Testament (OT)

The Old Testament of the Bible pictures 'The Ark' differently from the New Testament. The Ark in the Old Testament appeared on three different occasions:

(1) It appeared as an **Ark of Salvation** unto Noah and his family,

(2) As **an Ark of preservation** unto Moses in childhood,

(3) As **an Ark of the Covenant** between God and Israel (Genesis 6:9-22, Exodus 2:3, Exodus 25:16-22), where it was designed to lead Israel in her journey to the Promised Land. Not only that, it resided with them when they settled in the land. It represented God's presence in the Israelite's journey, in war and in worship. (Exodus 25:16-22, Exodus 40, 1 Samuel 4:1-11, 1 Chronicles 15:1, Joshua 4:1-24.)

Conclusion: The Ark in the Old Testament has its true picture in the New Testament. It was visible in the Old Testament and could be carried only by the Levites. But in the New Testament, it is spiritual and resides in the heart of every believer in Jesus Christ.

QUESTIONS

1. What can you picture from the fact that God initiated the Ark for worship (Genesis 6:14-22) while man imitated the Ark in the form of religion (Exodus 2:1-3)?
2. What should be our attitudes as Christians towards the Ark, which symbolizes God the Holy Spirit? (1 Corinthians 6:19).
3. Enumerate the importance of the Ark in believers' life.

Notes

Study Two

THE ARK (PART 2)

MEMORY VERSE: *"That Christ dwells in your heart through faith, that you, being rooted and grounded in love, may be able to comprehend with all the saints"* (Ephesians 3:17, 18).

BIBLE PASSAGE: *Hebrews 9:1-28*

INTRODUCTION

In the first part of this study, we learned that the Old Testament (OT) pictures the Ark differently from the New Testament (NT), and thus, we learned about the OT perspective of the Ark.

In this study, we shall consider the second part, which is the Ark in the New Testament. In our Bible passage (Hebrews 9:1-28) this week, we are brought to the knowledge of how the NT ark functions through our Lord Jesus Christ. It unfolded the mysteries surrounding Christ as the Ark knocking on the door of our hearts to have a permanent stay, just as the Ark did in Israel (Revelation 3:30).

Outlines:

1. The Ark in the New Testament (NT)
2. The Necessity of The Ark to Us As Believers

THE ARK IN THE NEW TESTAMENT (NT)

Little do we read of the wooden Ark in the New Testament. The birth of Jesus Christ, our Lord, and His bid for the Holy Spirit gradually affected the place of the wooden Ark. This became possible when Jesus Christ as the only means of salvation and the Holy Spirit indwelling the believers supplanted the functions performed by the Old Testament Ark.

The Old Testament Ark contained the items which are: rod of Aaron: which typifies Christ's spiritual guidance as a good Shepherd; the pot of manna, which explains Jesus Christ as the word of God that gives spiritual strength and life to those who believe in Him, and then, the two tables of the law, which shows Christ as the fulfilment of the law and the rules of conduct conditioned for entrance into the Kingdom of God. John 10:1-18, 1:1-14, 14:6, 6:35, Mark 10:17-21.

Jesus Christ is the Ark of God in which the secret of the eternal purpose is hidden. Therefore, we can discover, work on, and fulfil our eternal purpose through Jesus Christ. Once we have Christ, we have the secret of God, which is kept with those that fear Him (Psalms 25:14), and the presence of God put together. (John 14:20, 4:4, 1 Corinthians 6:19, 20, John 17, 23)

THE NECESSITY OF THE ARK TO US AS BELIEVERS

Every believer needs the Ark to live by. If you have not been in contact with it, then you have not yet become a Christian. You may bear names like James, John, and Paul, or be committed to Church activities, if Christ, **The Ark,** is not in you, you are worse than an infidel.

Just as **The Ark** saved Noah and his family from the flood, Moses from death in the river, and the Israelites through the wilderness, leading us to believe that God was in their midst, so also is Jesus Christ, The Ark, in the New Testament performs the work of salvation, redemption, leading, sanctification, intercession, warfare, etc., in the life of every believer. He is our power, our life, and the presence of God's character in us. John 3:16, 17.

Now, for **The Ark** to reside in you, you must, at first, enter into it. Jesus is **The Ark** of Salvation. If you accept Him, He will enter into you to stay forever. Do you know what? Once you have Him, you have peace, victory, and joy for evermore.

Why not enter the Ark today? He is knocking to come into you. Tomorrow may be too late!

Conclusion: *Just as in the days of Noah, people were implored perhaps for days, months or years to join the Ark and be saved from the flood. Today, I beseech you to enter into Jesus Christ, the only Ark through which any nation can be saved from the coming tribulations and death in hell. Since Noah's Ark was only one to save the world of* *his time, the way of salvation today has no duplicate. Don't be deceived! John 14:6.*

QUESTIONS

1. Relate the functions of Noah's Ark with the work Jesus is doing among humankind.
2. Why do you think people reject Christ today, and what explanation do you have for their objections?
3. Was salvation through Jesus only for humankind? Explain convincingly with the aid of Scriptures.
4. What answer do you have for other religious groups claiming we are serving the same God and why?

Notes

Study Three

THE FLOATING ARK

MEMORY VERSE: *"But the LORD God called unto the man, 'Where are you?'"* (Genesis 3:9).

BIBLE PASSAGE: Genesis 7:17-24

INTRODUCTION

Originally, **The Ark** of Noah was not built to save him and his family alone. Our God is not wicked. The Ark was fashioned to save the entire world of that time, i.e., those who might believe the words of Noah that there would be a flooding of the entire world. **The Ark** was big enough to contain both man and animals living at that time.

However, because of pleasure and continual admiration of evil, many ignored the warning and chose to perish with the flood instead of identifying with the 'stupidity' of Noah, when he said what had never happened would happen. (Matthew 24:37-39).

This idiocy of presumptuous negligence multiplied their sins by way of (1) disbelieving God and his prophets (2 Chronicles 20:20 John 14:1), (2) being in love with the world and all its lust (John 2: 15-17), (3) disobedience and deterrence from the divine guidance and instructions (Ephesians 2:2, 5:6, Romans 5:19, 2 Corinthians 10:6). In a similar vein today, we add to our sins by rejecting Christ, the only way to saving the world. (John 3:17-21).

Outlines:

1. Ark on the water
2. Why Jesus may wander in your life

ARK ON THE WATER

The Ark of Noah floated when the water prevailed and greatly increased on the earth. As a result, all living things perished without

9

remedy, Genesis 7:17-24. Such is the destruction that comes when the Ark floats in someone's life.

Water may indeed typify God's word, but in some other cases, it reveals the appearance of evil and sin. (Revelation 12:15, Ezekiel.7:17, Psalms 88:16, 17)

Regardless of your status, if this water (a symbol of evil and sin) overflows in your spirit, the Ark will float, for it does not yoke with sin. Consequently, the end attracts destruction. Many people claim they are Christians, but the Lord Jesus Christ is not rooted in them. Christ in them is like the Ark of Noah wandering on the surface of water.

Why Jesus May Wander in your Life

On our own, we can do absolutely nothing in the world described by Victor Slatter as a "dog-eats-dog environment". Except for when we allow Jesus to come and pitch His tent and dwell forevermore in us, we are like vessels which hold no water. You can imitate someone, but you cannot be as exactly as he is. Nevertheless, to be as exactly as Christ is, i.e. having the same character, thought, and worldview as Christ, it must not be by imitation but by implantation. Thus, you must die for God, who is the Spirit to take up your body, and by so doing, you will become like Christ. (Romans 8:9-17).

If that is not the case with you, then the following may be the reasons why Jesus Christ is wandering in your life:

  i.   An increasingly sinful life (Psalms 66:18),
  ii.   Inappropriate or lack of devotion and communication with God (Revelation 3:20),
  iii. Lack of knowledge,
  iv.   Faithlessness (Hebrews 11:6),
  v.   Worries and love for pleasure, (Mark. 4:18, 19, 1 John 2:15-17),
  vi.   Indecision and idolatry (2 Corinthians 6:14-16),
  vii. Blasphemy (saying what is not right about God). (Mark. 3:28, 29),
  viii. Lack of godly concern for other creatures (Genesis 2:15) etc.

Conclusion: *When the unpleasant water overflowed in Adam and Eve, God wandered around the garden, looking for where to rest and communicate with them. (Genesis 3:8, 9). The same happened when God wandered upon Balaam's water but found rest in the heart of a donkey (Numbers 22:21-30). You are not a Christian when God is not in you, and speaking with you.*

QUESTIONS

1. List other things that may cause God to wander in people's lives even when they claim to be Christians.
2. What can you do to prevent what is listed in Question 1 from happening in your life?

Notes

Study Four

THE CAPTURED ARK

MEMORY VERSE: *"Finally, my brethren, be strong in the Lord and in the power of His might"* (Ephesians 6:10).

BIBLE PASAGE: *1 Samuel 4:1-11*

INTRODUCTION

How would you feel if, as a wife, you are alone facing the beating in an escalating confrontation against a family of ten; all of a sudden, your husband appeared and a smile of relief flickers across your face because you thought that with the presence of your husband the beating would subside; on the contrary, the beating continued even more severely in the presence of your husband, who folded his arms, saying he is not going to fight?

I so much love the way Dr Kwakpovwe Chris puts it. He said:

"It's a tragedy because divine heritage was turned to divine humiliation. It is the story of the day divine honour was turned into divine shame, and supernatural glory was turned to demonic groaning; while a people of miracle were turned to a people of ridicule! It was the day when the destined loser (the Philistines) became the winner because the destined winner (the Jews) quit, while the loser (the Philistines) simply refused to quit."

Israelites were not the fright of other nations, 'The Ark,' or God, in their midst was. When the children of Israel sensed the sustained and uncontrollable onslaught coming from their opponent, they thought it was imperative to bring the Ark to the battlefront to reverse the defeat coming to their camp. When Eli's children came with the Ark, the Philistines became frightened knowing what the Ark stood for and thus, were casting woes upon themselves, crying, and regretting coming in battle against the Israelites.

Unfortunately, they summoned courage and fought the Israelites to flee, even in the presence of the Ark of power. Not only did they overcome the Israelites, but the Ark of Power also became their target and was captured.

Outlines:

1. The Spiritual Battle of Christians
2. The Enemies Within

THE SPIRITUAL BATTLE OF CHRISTIANS

Christian Life is a battlefield, and every believer is expected to put on the whole armour of God and become non-retreating soldiers (Ephesians 6:10-18). We fight to protect our lives, assignments, the purpose of God, and the Headship of Christ, which always are the targets in any spiritual war. In any war, people fight mostly to incapacitate, ruin pleasure, get the spoils, and capture people involved in the battle and their territories (Mark 3:27, John 10:10).

Similarly, Satan and his cohorts fight to manipulate, intimidate, and dominate the life and affairs of the Christian who desires to live for God. This, therefore, prepares the ground on which we must fight. Only Christians with 'the Ark' inside can be sure of victory at the end because, apart from Him (Christ, the Ark), "we can do nothing" (John 15:5).

We must not forget, moreover, that our enemies know the source of our power. They know without God, we are powerless, and that is why they make us sin in order to capture 'the Ark' from the inside of us. They want to deter us from our source of power before projecting attacks into our lives. Once 'the Ark' is gone, their victim is left without immunity; meaning the Christian will become "Ichabod" (the departure of God's glory for protection -- I Samuel 4:21-22).

THE ENEMIES WITHIN

A Yoruba adage quotes, "If the household death does not kill, the one outside cannot kill." Before your spiritual enemy projects attacks into your life, it will, first of all, study to have full knowledge of your strengths and weaknesses. Once that is done, it will capitalize on your weaknesses to capture your strength. Your weaknesses are satanic agents living inside of you. They include anger, strife, malice, love of money, lust for strange women, drunkenness, and ungodly counsel etc.

If any of these is your attitude, then you have enemies within. Their sole responsibility is to open the closed door of your heart for easy penetration of the outward enemies to capture the Ark and thereafter oppress to make life unbearable for you.

'The Ark' is the **Holy Spirit.** Your constant disobedience and rebellion to His leadership could aftermath, snuff His presence out of your heart, and that could open you up for molestation, mutilation, and even death. Is 'the Ark' in you now (Judges 16, 1 Samuel 31)?

Conclusion: *"...The race is not to the swift or the battle to the strong..."* (Ecclesiastics. 9:11). Living for Jesus Christ in holiness is our power. If we allow this to be captured by our enemies, then we have nothing left but to flee before the enemies. Pray that God should eliminate the enemies within you and give you strength in the areas of your weaknesses.

QUESTIONS

1. Highlight the behaviours that may cause a Christian to flee before the enemies.
2. What can you do from your own angle to be on the winning side?

Notes

Study Five

THE ARK AND THE DAGON

MEMORY VERSE: *"Do not be yoked together with unbelievers. For what do righteousness and wickedness have in common? Or what fellowship can light have with darkness"* (2 Corinthians 6:14)?

BIBLE PASSAGE: 1 Samuel 5:1-12.2

INTRODUCTION

'The battle was fierce, and the Ark was captured', was our last lesson. Now, as a custom in Ashdod, the land of the Philistines, the most notorious enemy, when captured, was taken to the house of the gods in a way of giving glory to them for making victory possible.

This degrading circumstance was experienced by the Israelites on three different occasions: First was when Samson, who was considered a threat to the Philistines, was captured and was made to perform before Dagon after his eyes were gouged out (Judges 16:21-25). The Second was when King Saul died in a battle against the Philistines, and his armour and body were fastened to the temple of their idols. (1 Samuel 31:8-10). And lastly, when the Israelites were defeated, the Philistines captured the Ark from Ebenezer to Ashdod and set it side by side with the Dagon (meaning fish), their national idol (1 Samuel 5).

Outlines:

1. Why may the Ark be captured?
2. Setting the Ark **Side by Side** with the Dagon.

WHY THE ARK MAY BE CAPTURED

One may wonder, how on earth it could be possible for the Philistines to capture the Ark of God. Apart from human security, God Himself

17

protects the Ark always with the cloud in the morning, which typifies the glory of God, and fire in the night, which symbolizes the presence of the Holy Spirit (Exodus 40:34-38).

Likewise, in believers' life, the Ark is being protected in between the glory and the Spirit of God, which definitely cannot be so weak for the enemies' penetration (Acts 1:8, John 16:13a, John 14:15-21). But what then could have consequently made the enemies' approach so easy to capture the Almighty Ark?

Before any attempt to lay hands on the Ark, the enemies often ensure that the glory departs and the fire quenches so that it can easily be captured in that state of insecurity. The three major sins that often cause the departure and the quenching of such glory and fire, respectively, are:

1. **Disobedience:** King Saul disobeyed God, and the protection left him. (1 Samuel 15:10, 11, 16:14)
2. **Pride:** Samson was captured because of his pride. (Judges 16:16-20).
3. **Immoralities:** The Ark in Israel lost its protection and was captured by the Philistines because of the immoralities of the children of Eli (I Samuel 2:22-26).

SETTING THE ARK SIDE BY SIDE WITH THE DAGON

When the Ark completely loses control over you, other things left become the Dagon, which, in this context, is settling by the Ark in your life. Its main functions are to confuse you, cause doubt, and make you reject the headship of Christ over your life. Thereafter, he wants you to end up in hellfire because the effect of such confusion could result in backsliding or apostasy.

Your own Dagon may be money, fame, great passion for a position, drunkenness, idolatry, etc. Once you are into any of these as a Christian, you are settling the Ark side by side with the Dagon. The consequences of that could be pestilences, attacks from the enemies or even death (1 Sam 5:6-12).

Conclusion: *When the glory and the Spirit of God departs, the Ark eventually disappears, and what one is left with becomes madness,* *just like King Saul. How many of such "madness" can you see on pulpits today?*

QUESTIONS

1. List and explain some of the "madness" you can imagine in today's Church leaders and followers.
2. What can we do to bring back the lost glory of the contemporary Church? Will this revolution start from you? How?

Notes

Study Six

THE NEGLECTED ARK

MEMORY VERSE: *"because, although they knew God, they did not glorify Him as God, nor were thankful, but became futile in their thoughts, and their foolish hearts were darkened"* (Romans 1:21).

BIBLE PASSAGE: 1 Samuel 7:1 & 2, 1 Chronicle 13:3, Romans 1:18-22.

INTRODUCTION

After the Ark returned from the Philistines, it was ushered into the house of Abinadab and was forgotten for twenty years. Among those things, or the major reason why King Saul fumbled and died shamefully, was the fact that throughout his reign, he never consulted the Ark of God for any instruction. He neglected the ruling of the Ark, having Samuel as an alternative. Hence when Samuel died, he still found no reason for approaching the Ark to make any enquiry or to worship. He became arrogant that he saw himself as more important than the Ark, which was God-type.

Outlines:

1. Neglecting God's Ruling
2. Why God Must Rule

NEGLECTING GOD'S RULING

When a man desires a position of authority in the Church or in a society, he goes about seeking favour or even fasting and praying with humility in pretence. He says, "God! Use me! Send me!" Once he is sent, he becomes egocentric and never sees reasons why he should give the glory back to God or inquire about what is next to be done.

In this same scenario was Saul made a king? Perhaps, he had dreamed and prayed about it before having an encounter with the Prophet, who, through instruction from God, anointed him King over God's people

(Israel). At first, he was obedient, fearful and humble, but when he became the King, he never felt he needed to give the Kingdom back to God, the owner of His people. He became alien to instructions and never really saw the need for spiritual intervention in the affairs of the state governed by him. No thought for the Ark, let alone asking for its guidance.

The only time he felt he needed assistance after the demise of Prophet Samuel was when he was in trouble with the Philistines, and then, he sought an alternative for the Ark. He went to a woman with medium spirit (1 Sam 11:12-13, 15:28).

WHY GOD MUST RULE

All Kingdoms belong to God (Dan.5:21, Isaiah 37:16, 2 Chronicles 20:6) because He is All-knowing and Sovereign. He knows the end from the very beginning. Even though He appointed us, we do not know what He wants to achieve in the end. His purposes are revealed and fulfilled precept upon precept, line upon line, a little here, and a little there. (Psalms 119:27, Is 28:10, 13). If anyone must be engrossed in this divine program, there is need for total submission to God. Otherwise, you will be running the errand which you were not sent. How many of you are running the errand which you were not sent? Know this today, that it is a wasted effort which shall earn you no reward. Submit yourself to God today for worship and instructions so as not to weep bitterly as Saul, the King, wept.

Conclusion: *God gives responsibilities, as well as volition. Irrespective of man's volition, God desires to stay in the center circle of man's choices to activate them to accomplish His eternal purpose. Why not call for his intervention in all your activities today? You may know a purpose, but the reason for that purpose you do not know, only God knows.*

QUESTIONS

1. Name five occasions in the Bible where God, the Ark, was neglected and the consequences.
2. Relate these to your life, marriage and ministry. Are you yielding all or part to God's full interventions?

Notes

Study Seven

THE ARK OF JUDGMENT

MEMORY VERSE: *"by those who come near me, I must be regarded as holy, and before all the people, I must be glorified."* (Leviticus 10:3b)

BIBLE PASSAGES: *1 Chronicle 13:9, Leviticus 10:1-3*

INTRODUCTION

Love and holiness are God's popular characteristics. Each cannot work without the other. They cooperate even in God's dealings with humankind. It is greatly impossible for God to be holy without loving, and likewise, His holiness can never suppress His love. In His love dwells His judgement. Therefore, He judges us because He loves us (Revelation 3:19).

A father who admires his son so much cannot watch him spoil his valuable clothes with secretions. Rather, he will reprimand the child to show his disapproval for such a gloomy attitude. In a similar vein is God with his own children. Whenever His love draws us closer, we should not fail to consider His holiness, which cannot be toyed with. We cannot approach His Holiness with the filthiness of our hearts and actions (Leviticus 11:44).

Outlines:

1. Laws of the Ark
2. Why Uzzah must die
3. Judgement on Disobedience

LAWS OF THE ARK

God gave instructions ahead of coming closer to the Ark to avoid the loving Ark turned to judgement. He gave clear and detailed information to Moses concerning who bears Ark. This was designated to the clans and families of the Kohathite, a branch of the Levites. And also issued a warning that, even though they were the legitimate bearers of the Ark, they must not reach out their hands to touch the holy things of the Ark, or else they would die (Numbers 4:1-4, 15).

Although He loves and cherishes our fellowship, He is also serious about His instructions. He can be so friendly and generous, but no matter how useful or closer you may be to Him, He cannot bend His laws to fulfil your selfish desires.

The death of Nadab and Abihu (Leviticus 10:1-3) and Uzzah is a reflection that doing noble deeds in an ignoble manner indicates danger.

WHY UZZAH MUST DIE

Uzzah died not because he was unholy or because he was hated by God, but because he was made to sin against God's instructions. For that sole reason, he must die! His death was not only the consequence of his own disobedience but also of the sin of the entire nation of Israel because:

1. Uzzah was not a Kohathite. God's instruction was that only the Kohathite should be set aside for such duty (Numbers 4:4-15, 7:9).
2. The Ark was to be carried by a man and not a cart or any other animal (Exodus 25:14, 15, Numbers 4:5-8). The reasons for this are simple. A man rides on animals as an indication of dominion, and likewise, God must ride on man to show his supremacy over the dominionship of man. Man cannot subdue God by putting the Ark on a cart. If God and man ride on a cart, it shows that God only has dominion over other creatures and not man. It puts man's authority side by side with God's authority. Therefore, men must bear the Ark on themselves to show their submission and dependency on the Independence of God.
3. Human hand is prohibited from touching the Ark of Power. Power belongs to God without any human effort. Not even the Kohathites were permitted to touch the Ark (Numbers 4:15). The holiness of God must not be polluted by the sinful nature of man (Acts 17:25). Since Uzzah reached his hands to assist the power and holiness of God, he must surely die!

JUDGMENT ON DISOBEDIENCE

God's business requires seriousness. It must never be perfunctorily performed or done irreverently or in accordance with mere expediency (1 Samuel 6:19, 20). Drawing closer to God is not really the issue, but knowing fully the dos and don'ts of Him, whom you intend to draw closer to.

Even though you are intimate with God, you are not left out in His outbreak judgement if you disobey His instructions. We shall explain more about this in our subsequent lessons.

Conclusion: *Human constitutions can be amended, manipulated, or suppressed to favour a man of influence. But God cannot alter, bend or overlook His instructions just because somebody engages in His business. He magnifies His word above all His names (Psalms 138:2b (NKJV)). That is why judgement must start from those who call on His name (1 Peter 4:17).*

QUESTIONS

1. Why do you think judgement must start from the Church?
2. Write a short note on our memory verse today: Leviticus 10:3b.
3. Discuss other reasons why Uzzah must die.

Notes

Study Eight

THE ARK GIVEN AWAY

MEMORY VERSE: *"The crowd that followed kept shouting, away with him!"* (Acts 21:36)

BIBLE PASSAGES: *1 Chronicles 13:1-14, John 19:1-16.*

INTRODUCTION

David was furious when the Ark that was known to be the Ark of Joy suddenly became the Ark of Judgement and of death. He became frightened that he thought it was not right for him to dwell again with the Ark. Seeing himself as a sinner, he thought it was extremely dangerous to reside with the holiness of God. When he was not ready to die, he ordered that the Ark be 'Given away' to the house of a poor man whose death meant nothing to society after all. The King's expectation was dashed when the fearful Ark turned into a blessing in the house of Obed-Edom within three months.

Outlines:

1. Jesus: The Ark Given Away
2. The Replica of the event at Calvary

JESUS: The ARK Given Away

Jesus Christ, Our Lord, came in the flesh to dwell and show His perfect will unto us (humankind). He preached what had never been preached, and performed miracles beyond human imagination. His outstanding attributes cannot be overemphasized yet, all these seemed to mean nothing to the Chief Priests and a number of mobs following them. They ganged up and accused Him wrongfully before the earthly judge who, in his decision, demanded an answer about who he must release, between Jesus Christ, the good man, and Barabbas, the robber.

Maliciously, their agreement was that the robber should be released and, thus, gave up our Lord Jesus Christ to death. They thought it was over, but the dead welcomed Him and got the miracle of life in the Paradise as against the complication in Hell or shoel. Jesus, having become the Lord of the living, was the Ark which was given away only to also become the Lord of the dead (Romans 14:9, Matthew 22:32, John 5:25).

THE REPLICA OF THE EVENT AT CALVARY

Today, as a replica of the event at Calvary, many people think they have no need to accept Christ. They think the poor and the afflicted need Him the most. I was introduced to a man during 'Church on the move'. He insisted he doesn't need to accept Christ but introduced us to his sister, who has attained a marriageable age but has no one to marry, to join our Church youth program or even become a member.

So many ministers of God (so to say) preach the word of God with their hearts far from Him. If we go by the word they preach, we may be blessed by God while they themselves operate under the curse and the wrath of God to come. Have you ever seen a minister of God who prays for the sick, and they get well, but when his wife or children fall sick, he becomes so agitated that he consults different physicians for their healing? While seeking medical assistance is not abysmal to the Christian faith, the so-called minister of God may be doubting the power of God for the healing of his sick family. He may be 'giving away the Ark' to others equally in need of it, and God decides to honour His word and name.

When some preachers preach, people are blessed, but the preachers themselves remain in a worse situation. If the case is referring to you, it means you are 'giving away the Ark', which should also have become a blessing unto you.

Conclusion: *One can imagine the zeal of King David and his eventual disappointment and anger in bringing the Ark to his own country after God killed Uzzah. Zeal displayed contrary to God's instruction amount to disobedience. More so, "The Kingdom of God is not in word but in power." (1 Corinthians 4:20). If we must bring people to faith, we must be careful that we are not 'giving away the Ark', i.e. Christ, in a way of preaching what we are not practising. Preach,* *using your personal experience, so that God will honour not only His word but also the preacher (James 1:22-25).*

QUESTIONS

1. List ten qualities of a good preacher.
2. What danger lies in preaching what you are not practising?

Support your answer with biblical references.

Notes

Study Nine

THE SETTLED ARK

MEMORY VERSE: *"...if anyone hears my voice and opens the door, I will come in and eat with him and he with me."* (Revelation 3:20 (NIV)

BIBLE PASSAGE: Genesis 8:1-4

INTRODUCTION

After one hundred and fifty days of wandering and tottering, the Ark of Noah rested on the mount of Ararat. After fifty-four days, Noah and his family opened the door of the Ark and worshipped the awesomeness of God.

Jesus, the Ark, is longing to rest in man's soul. He is wandering at the door for whosoever is willing to open that He may eat and drink with Him (Revelation 3:20). He died for this and was crucified at the centre, typifying the area where Christ must be positioned in our lives, i.e. at the centre of our heart. Not our mouth, head or hands. We must make Him the Lord of our conscience. As the 'Yoruba' calls it, "Eri Okan", meaning "God of the Heart". He must rule over your life for you to be like Him. He cannot force Himself in just as the Ark did not force itself into the sanctuary. It was carried with human hands. So also, the decision to open the door of your heart for Him to come in is solely your own responsibility.

Outlines:

Prerequisites for a Settled Ark

PREREQUISITES FOR A SETTLED ARK

For the Ark (Christ) to permanently settle in the tabernacle (your heart), a few things must be done on your part:

1. Preparation I Chronicles 15:1

King David did not just go for the Ark. He had, first of all, prepared a temple for it in **HIS OWN CITY**. The Ark cannot rest outside the temple or in another man's city. If this happens, your blessing becomes another man's (1 Chronicles 13).

Don't only tell people about Jesus. Allow Him first into your life. Prepare his temple in your own body, allow Him to have a peaceful stay, and so shall your life be endowed with His blessing (I Corinthians 6:19, 2 Corinthians 6:16-18).

2. Ministry of the Levites (the chosen ones) 1 Chronicles 15:2

David learned his lesson the hard way through the death of Uzzah and, thereafter, had a change of mind and called for the Levites to bear the Ark out of the house of Obed-Edom to his own city. The Levites are the custodians of God's word and the ministers of the Holy Spirit today. They may be Pastors, workers or members of the true Church of God. They are the people chosen to minister the undiluted word of God with an exemplary lifestyle. They are simply the Disciples of Christ (Matthew 10, Matthew 28:1620, Acts 1:8).

Now, it is not everybody that preaches the true word of God. Some are called by their belly, just like Uzzah bore the Ark on contract.

Only those who are chosen by God have the true word, which can usher the Ark (Jesus Christ) into your body temple (your heart) because, they have more knowledge about God (1 Chronicles 15:12, 13).

3. Creating Awareness: I Chronicles 15:3

David called the attention of all the children of Israel to his intention to bring the Ark back into the temple. He did not hide it among only the elders. We are to make our newly accepted faith known to all people. We must not hide our faith for fear of persecution. Let the whole world know that you have now declared to live for Christ (Matthew 5:14-16, Matthew 10:32, 33).

4. Appointment of Singers: 1 Chronicles 15:16

"Enter his gates with thanksgiving and his court with praise, give thanks to him and praise his name" (Psalms 100:4).

David understood the necessity of being joyful in bringing the Ark into its sanctuary. He employed singers to sing and rejoice before it. We are not to be forced or deceived into accepting Christ or into responding to the altar calls. Jesus must be celebrated in our hearts, not just tolerated, and the decision to do this is solely ours because we own our choices. That is the only property we own on earth. Not even God can force a choice on us, and that is why He waits outside for us to exercise our volition in bringing Jesus Christ into our hearts. This must be done with a gladsome mind.

5. Appointment of gatekeepers I Chronicles 15:17, 18, 23, 24

As a matter of urgency, the Ark needs security to avoid any further takeover by the enemies. David did this too. Once we accept Jesus Christ as our Lord and Saviour, we need security like, shunning ungodly meetings, separation from ungodly friends, eschewing listening to ungodly music and watching pornographic films, etc.

These are the only ways we can keep our hearts away from intruders. (Matthew 12:34, 35, Proverbs 27:29, Ephesians 5:19, Colossians 3:16).

6. Judgement on the Mockers I Chronicles 15:29, 2 Samuel 6:20-23

After David danced almost naked before the Ark, Michel, his wife, despised him. She incurred God's wrath never to bear children. Surely, when you declare the territory of your life for the headship of Christ, mockers will rise from among the people who enjoyed your sloppy cause to hellfire. They may be former friends, colleagues, family, relations, etc. Do not take notice of their criticism, God will take care of them. (Exodus 14:13, 14, 2 Timothy 3:12, 13).

7. Fellowship Offering 1 Chronicles 16:1-2

David did not just bring the Ark into its sanctuary, he also offered fellowship offerings before the Ark. You did well by accepting Jesus

Christ as your Lord and Saviour, but that should not be the end. It is mostly important that you fellowship with the new Lord you have just accepted. This must be done through spending quality time in His presence, studying His word (the Bible), praying and attending church programmes. (2 Timothy 3:14-17, 2 Timothy 2, 15, 16).

Conclusion: *We have finally come to the conclusion of our study on the Ark. More importantly, let us bring it into our lives and keep the Ark of God through which only we can be saved.*

QUESTIONS

1. What do you need Jesus Christ for?
2. How often must you fellowship with Him?
3. How best can you let Him be in the controlling circle of your heart?

Notes

Study Ten

DANGERS OF BACKSLIDING

MEMORY VERSE: Jesus replied, *"No one who puts his hand to the plough and looks back is fit for service in the Kingdom of God"* (Luke 9:62).

BIBLE PASSAGE: Jeremiah 2:14-19, Jeremiah 3:11-25

INTRODUCTION

The kingdom was divided into two parts after King Solomon: the northern kingdom of Israel and the southern kingdom of Judah. However, Jerusalem, the Temple, and the Davidic royal line were all in Judah. Both kingdoms sinned by worshipping idols, but Israel was worse. God sent prophets to both kingdoms to warn them. God warned Israel that Assyria would be used to punish them (e.g., Isaiah 10:5-6), and Assyria did indeed capture Israel in 722 BC. Assyria nearly captured Judah as well, but God intervened (Isaiah 36–37). The punishment meted out to Israel should have served as a warning to Judah to repent of their idolatry. However, they deteriorated as they pretended to believe in God while pursuing idols (Isaiah 29:13). This was considered treachery by God. God forewarned Judah. God warned Judah that Babylon would be used to punish Judah, just as Assyria was used to punish Israel (e.g. Isaiah 39:6, Jeremiah 20:4).

Outlines:

1. What is Backsliding?
2. Some causes of Backsliding
3. Dangers of Backsliding

WHAT IS BACKSLIDING?

Backsliding is a combination of two English words, 'back' and 'slide'. The word 'back' means returning or moving in the opposite direction to the one in which you had earlier faced. While 'slide' is a smooth, quiet and gradual change of attitude without trying to stop yourself.

Backsliding, therefore, means returning to the deeds or things you had earlier agreed or promised not to do. It is, perhaps due to the pressure or the pleasure you are enjoying from it. It is forsaking the Truth without necessarily accusing it.

There are two different words: Accusing the Truth you once believed - APOSTASY (Hebrews 6:4-5) and manifesting a disloyal attitude to the Truth you once embraced without necessarily condemning it - BACKSLIDING (Romans 1:8-21).

Backsliding occurs in the heart and reflects in the actions (Jeremiah 3:10, Proverbs 14:14, Jeremiah 3:6). Effort must be made to reconcile a backslider with God; more effort is needed to bring the apostates back to God (Ezekiel. 18:26, Ezekiel. 3:30).

SOME CAUSES OF BACKSLIDING

On the part of the Church:

1. Falsifying the Truth of the gospel in a bid to win souls (Galatians 1:6-10, Galatians 2:1-5).
2. When the new birth is not considered before putting people in the position of service or when people are enticed with positions in the Church (John 3:35).
3. Inadequate or poor visitation (1 Corinthians 11:34, 16:10, 2 Corinthians 1:15, 12:20).
4. Disappointment in ministers and church workers (Matthew 5:16, 2 Timothy 3:2 Corinthians 10:5).
5. Unsound biblical teaching (2 Timothy 2:15, 3:16).
6. Harsh disciplines imposed on the offenders (Read about Onesimus: Philemon 8-21).
7. Strict rules or orders of the Church without letting people know why they must comply, and disapproving people's exercise of volition even though some may be guided (Romans 6:14, Romans 11:6, Galatians 5:4).

On the part of the Backslider:

1. The love of pleasure rather than the things of God (1 John 2:15-17, 1 Timothy 5:6, James 5:1-5).
2. Looking up to humans instead of Jesus Christ (Hebrews 12:1 & 2).

3. Impatience in time of crisis (2 Timothy 2:3, 10, 2 Timothy 4:5, James 5:11, 1 Thessalonians 5:14, James 5:7&8, Ecclesiastics 7:8).
4. Lack of knowledge of growing spiritual life (Proverbs 1:7, Proverbs 2:3-6, 8:10, 12:1, 15:14, 1 Samuel 2:3).
5. Lack of fellowship with God (I Corinthians 1:9, Acts 2:42, Philippians 3:10, 2:182, 1 John 1:7).
6. Regular absence from Church due to job demands (Ecclesiastics 1:2-4).

DANGERS OF BACKSLIDING

On the part of the Church (when backsliding becomes rampant):

1. It displays spiritual famine, and how quickly the Church needs spiritual meals and revival.
2. It affects the spiritual steadfastness of the Church.
3. It opens the Church up to external attacks.
4. It can give evil names to the Church, i.e. bring about a bad reputation.
5. It can lead to the fall of innocent men when not wisely dealt with.
6. It can make the Church a synagogue of Satan, i.e. brings about the backsliding of the whole congregation, which thereafter may lead to doom.
7. It depopulates the Kingdom of God and the entire body of the Church.

On the part of the Backslider:

1. It leads to committing more sins against God.
2. It makes God wrathful.
3. It opens one up to satanic attacks.
4. It withholds good from the person or people involved (Jeremiah 5:26).
5. It leads to hellfire.

Conclusion: *Backsliding is an act that God passionately abhors and judges, especially when it is caused by people who are supposed to live by example.*

QUESTIONS

1. What must churches do to prevent backsliding? Explain in full detail.
2. Can the society, government, culture, or traditions contribute to backsliding in the Church? How?

Notes

Study Eleven

DANGERS OF BACKSLIDING PART 2

MEMORY VERSE: *"For Demas, because he loved the world, has deserted me and has gone to Thessalonica. Crescens has gone to Galatia and Titus to Dalmatia"* (2 Timothy 4:10).

BIBLE PASSAGE: Numbers 16:1-50

INTRODUCTION

Korah, Dothan and Abram considered Moses' instruction as burdensome and domineering. This is because they were Levites too, but were not priests. They seemed to dislike the idea that the Aaron's family should hold the priesthood in the highest regard. They argued that everyone was sacred and that sacrifices should be made by everyone, including them (v.3). They questioned and disapproved of Moses' authority over them. This insurrection against the priests and their government was joined by 250 of Israel's princes and leaders (v.2). Moses sent orders to Korah and his rebellious group to settle the dispute. When Moses called them out of their tent, Dathan and Abiram refused and condemned Moses' leadership instead. These men, alluding to the earlier promise made in (Exodus 3:8) that God would lead them into "a land flowing with milk and honey", were grumbling (in a sarcastic manner) that Moses had led them away from a land flowing with milk and honey (Egypt) and brought them into a desert. The idea was that, after Moses failed to keep his word, he was now attempting to deceive the populace by hiding his failure or his genuine intentions. Therefore, they thought it was right to silence him once and for all. Unfortunately, God intervened, and they died unexpectedly.

Outlines:

1. Identifying who could be a Backslider
2. Healing the Backslider

IDENTIFYING WHO COULD BE A BACKSLIDER

1. He disputes what is widely known as the Truth of God's word.
2. He picks offences in sermons and leaders.
3. He does things in his own way and not in a Biblical way.
4. He presumptuously absences himself from Church meetings without genuine reason or prior notification. Even if he is a Church worker.
5. He dodges the Pastor, as well as other members, and lies about his whereabouts.
6. He may decide to live far away from where he can be identified with the Church or even Christ.
7. He hates being visited.
8. He criticizes discipline and does not forgive easily.
9. He withdraws from Church's responsibilities, especially Evangelism. He prefers to be an ordinary church member.
10. He gossips and speaks evil of other members.

HEALING THE BACKSLIDER

What the Church can do:

1. Pray earnestly against the spirit of backsliding in the Church because it is the work of Satan to draw people back to himself.
2. Visit the backslider often.
3. Study the word of God with them and make them feel that Christ still loves and died for them.
4. Don't overlook any misconduct in the Church. Judge and discipline the offenders in humility and love to deter other members from doing the same.

To the backslider:

1. Genuine repentance is important
2. Cultivate a fasting & prayerful life
3. Study God's word on a daily basis
4. Attend and be punctual at Church meetings
5. Seek spiritual guidance and counselling
6. Endure discipline
7. Disclose your identity as a child of God anywhere you find yourself

8. Bid goodbye to worldly friends and move on with growing Christian colleagues
9. Get a prayer partner you can confide in
10. War against the spirit of backsliding

Call to Return: No matter how far you might have gone, how more sinful you might have become, God is calling you to return to Him today because He loves you still (Jeremiah 3:12-15, Isaiah 1:18, Hos. 14:4, Romans 5:8-11, Jeremiah 4:4, 14).

QUESTIONS

1. What can the Church do to bring nations back to God?
2. Do you wish to return and stay forever in God? What are you doing now to perfect that?

Notes

Study Twelve

APPROPRIATE WORSHIP

MEMORY VERSE: *"Yet a time is coming and has now come when the true worshippers will worship the Father in spirit and in truth, for they are the kind of worshippers the Father seeks"* (John 4:23).

BIBLE PASSAGE: Revelation 15:2-4, 4:6-11

INTRODUCTION

Man's problem is not what to worship but how to worship. Without controversy, every human has got the idea deep in the soul that God does exist and needs to be worshipped. Atheists are inclusive because they likewise worship. Judging by the eternal purpose, all things are created for His pleasure (Revelation 4:11b). 'Pleasure' here means a feeling of happiness, satisfaction or enjoyment. Man must gladden God's heart in worship, and this, he fulfils whether he knows it or not.

Although there may be false or true worship, the idea of worship and the knowledge of God is hard-wired deeply in man's soul right from his creation. (Romans 1:18-22).

Outlines:

1. Man's attitude to worship
2. Religion and Worship

Man's Attitude to Worship

In anticipation to be independent of God, man has made a tireless effort to put aside anything called worship. If worship were eyes, then man would have plucked it out. If it were a hand then man would have amputated it, only to replace it with artificial. But God, who is Omniscient (All knowing), has made worship adhesive to the soul that both can never be separated in any way. With the mind, man thinks, with the heart, man incubates, with the soul, man relates to God in worship. The position of the soul is like that of a vehicle which

46

conveys you to your desired destination. Your soul brings you closer to God in worship.

Now, it is possible for a child to denounce his father, but not to the extent of flushing the chemical substance that formed him (the child) out of his own (the child's) body system. On that similar ground, you may oppose, rebel, or change objects in worship, but not to the level of refraining from it. Thus, when man found avoidance of worship complicated, they turned to religion instead.

RELIGION AND TRUE WORSHIP

In Acts 17:15-28, Paul addressed a group of very religious people in Athens:

"Ye men of Athens, I perceive that in things ye are too superstitious."

He had noticed that they worshipped many gods, and to be on the safe side, they had even erected a shrine to an "Unknown God". It is important to note that religion is not necessarily the worship of the Almighty God. It is part of Satan's strategy to counterfeit God's system of the "God-Man" relationship.

Religion has no root in God. It is an idea which originated from the mother-son Religion at Babel (Genesis 10:8-10) in 2247 BC. It is holding in reverence to someone or something. The object of worship varies according to custom, nationality, individual desire for holiness, fear, and superstition, or simply out of the search for the Truth. Religion is never God's intention, however, it is brought into Christianity by those who could not distinguish between carnal life and spiritual life and/or materialism and spiritualism. In trying to be religious, we knowingly or unknowingly worship many gods.

On the contrary, worship is never man's idea. It originated from Heaven and commanded on earth. It is God's way of relating to man and the entire creation. Unlike in Religion where it is "God, this is how I want to serve you," worship is, "Man, this is how I want to be reverenced." (Revelation 4:8-11, Exodus 40:116, Zechariah 2:11, Revelation 7:11-12).

Worship draws you closer to God and continues even after the demise of a man, but religion makes you embrace other gods in disguise of true worship. It separates you from God and does not continue after you die.

Conclusion: *Religion is contrary to God's will for man because in it man acts based on his own will. But in worship, all instructions come from God. In Religion, you manifest or say what truly you are not, but because worship is from the soul, you act outwardly what your inner man truly is.*

QUESTIONS

1. Give reasons why Religion is not True Worship.
2. Narrate the events that led to the emergence of religion at Babel, considering the mother-son religion of Semiramis.

Notes

1st QUARTERLY REVIEW

1. Compare the Ark in the Old Testament to the Ark in the New Testament.
2. According to Exodus 2:3, Explain what you understand by the Ark.
3. Among the Israelites, which tribe was appointed to carry the Ark?
4. Why do you, as a Christian, need the Ark?
5. What are the reasons why the Ark became the target of the Philistines?
6. Why was it possible for the Ark to be captured by the philistines?
7. Why do you think King Saul died shamefully?
8. Explain in brief why God desired men to carry the Ark and not animals.
9. In lesson 9, what are the prerequisites for a settled Ark?
10.
    a) How can you identify a backslider?
    b) What can the Church do to heal a backslider?
    c) What can a backslider do on his /her own to return to God?
11. What is True Worship? How can we truly worship?

Study Thirteen

APPROPRIATE WORSHIP (PART 2)

MEMORY VERSE: *"Now therefore, if you will indeed obey my voice and keep my covenant, then you shall be a special treasure to me above all people, for all the earth is mine"* (Exodus 19:5).

BIBLE PASSAGES: Exodus 3:7-12, Exodus 19

INTRODUCTION

Just like the plants desire photosynthesis, sheep desire green pasture, and men desire good food and water, so also, God desires True worship.

- He initiated it (Genesis 3:8), He respects it (Genesis 4:4),
- He raises leaders across nations and generations because of it (Exodus 3:1-6, Jeremiah 1:4-5),
- He loves it (Genesis 5:24),
- He gave conditions for it (Deuteronomy 28:1-14),
- He is jealous for it (Exodus 20:1-6),
- He delivers people because of it (Exodus 3:7-11),
- He turns men to it and forgives them because of it (Jeremiah 3:11-18), He is hungry for it, (Matthew 11:28-30),
- He gives rewards for it (Isaiah 1:19),
- He became human because of it (John 1:14),
- He died for it (John 10:11, 15, 17), And He can kill because of it (Leviticus 10:1-3, Jonah 1-4, Acts 5:1-11).

Outlines:

1. Why God desires True worship?
2. How does God want to be worshipped?

WHY GOD DESIRES TRUE WORSHIP

One may wonder why God so desires true worship that He can send people to hellfire because of it, and even in the Hell, all knees must still bow in worship (Philippians 2:10). The reasons are mainly because:

1. God wants reverence for His Supremacy (Exodus 20:1-3),
2. He wants to receive all the glory (Exodus 20:4-6),
3. He wants honour for His name (Exodus 20:7),
4. Worship is part of the eternal purpose (Exodus 20:8-11),
5. He desires the fellowship of His creation (Exodus 20:12),
6. He wants to preserve our life (Exodus 20:13),
7. He wants to secure peace and tranquility among His creation (Exodus 20:14),
8. He desires to protect our properties as they are given by Him as aids to fulfil our divine assignments (Exodus 20:15),
9. He wants to establish His Truth among us (Exodus 20:16, John 8:32, John 14:6),
10. He wants to maintain goodwill, good conduct etc., among His creation (Exodus 20:17).

HOW DOES GOD WANT TO BE WORSHIPPED?

Man misses it all when he says, "In my heart is my faith. I will worship God my own way, anyhow". No! No! No! You cannot worship God in your own way or anyhow. That can only show that you are being religious, and religion takes you nowhere beyond earthly recognition. You cannot say to your employer, 'I will do the job my own way or anyhow'. Your own way might not be the best, and anyhow is no how.

You must worship God in God's own way, according to His statutes. Because He initiated it and knows how best He wants it. That is why He gives instructions concerning how He wants it done. Failure to comply with these makes you a rebel that needs to be taught appropriate worship by force in hellfire. Yes! Hellfire. Satan shall be their teacher because he was once a worshipper in heaven. He knows how best to worship God (Ezekiel. 28:1-19, Isaiah 14:12). However, the worship shall no longer be rewarding but shall be as a matter of compulsion. The following are God's way to true worship.

1. Worship in Spirit and in Truth

2. Worship God in Holiness
3. Worship in fairness to God, man and other living creatures. Kill no man or animal for sacrifice.
4. Worship according to Biblical guidelines.
5. Worship based on Christ only.
6. Worship without pretence or as a matter of compulsion.
7. Worship in love towards God and man.
8. Worship with a gladsome mind and a heart focused on God.
9. Worship shows a good example of a lifestyle to follow.
10. Worship with fear and trembling for God, not man.
11. Worship by fulfilling our Lord's great commission.

Conclusion: *No other thing is right and good than to worship God exactly the way He wants to be worshipped.*

QUESTIONS

1. What do you think is the reason why God rejected Cain's sacrifice?
2. Do you think your worship is appropriate enough? Give reasons for your answer.

Notes

Study Fourteen

APPROPRIATE WORSHIP (PART 3)

MEMORY VERSE: *"God is Spirit, and his worshippers must worship Him in spirit and in truth"* (John 4:24).

BIBLE PASSAGE: John 4:20-24

INTRODUCTION

Worshipping in the spirit does not mean worshipping through imagination. It simply means being carried along by the one whom you worship or walking with God. Moreover, it is acting based on the divine instructions or being in the right mind of him that you worship. So many of us are not conscious of the God we serve. We do not really see Him in our minds. What we are fond of is being a copy of what others were instructed to do. Many do not have direct access to God, and the instructions to others may not be appropriate in your own worship of God. What do I mean? Already, the foundation for worship had been laid, which is Christ but to further build on Him, you need instructions from God Himself (1 Corinthians 3:10-15).

Outline:

Worship God in 'Spirit' and in 'Truth'

WORSHIP GOD IN SPIRIT AND IN TRUTH

"God is Spirit and they that worship Him must worship in 'Spirit' and in 'truth'" (John 4:24). We must recognize that a person has a spirit and a corporeal essence (John 3:6). Otherwise, we can refer to it as the 'Natural man' and the 'Spiritual man'. The primary reason why many newly converted people, after exulting in their new-found optimism, abruptly realise that their old fleshly desires still exist and begin to doubt their conversion is that they are unaware of our 'dual nature'. The 'natural man' cannot relate to God in his depraved state because of his dimly lit mind, which prevents him from grasping spiritual things. His understanding is also terribly wicked (Ephesians 4:14,

55

Jeremiah 17:9, Romans 8:7-8, I Corinthians 2:14, Mark 7:21-22, Ephesians 2:1, Romans 7:18).

Just as the Ethiopians cannot change their skin colour or a leopard change his spots, a natural man also cannot alter his character without supernatural assistance (Isaiah 13:23). So, if you want to worship God naturally then you are not a true worshipper but rather a religious person who serves an unlimited number of gods. God is Spirit, and if we are to worship Him, we must do so in Spirit and in Truth. The 'Spirit' is the Holy Spirit, and the 'truth' is Jesus Christ, the Word of God (John 14:6, 1 Pet. 1:23, James 1:18).

When man is said to be reborn, it means his spirit, once working alone, now got a renewal by clinging to the Holy Spirit, the Spirit of God, and the word of Christ to be directed in the wills of God. When the Holy Spirit witnesses with your spirit, your worship is appropriate, otherwise, inappropriate. Walking with God means walking in the Spirit, according to the word (Truth) of God. To walk with God, you must overcome the flesh, the natural man, by way of:

1. **AMPUTATION:** *"If thy hand or thy foot offends thee, cut them off"* (Matt. 18:8-9 (KJV)). Not literally, but if thy hand causes thee to steal, stop at once, make it not gradual. If thy foot causeth thee to go to the haunts of sin, stop short as if you were footless. *"If thine eye offends thee, causeth thee to look upon a woman to lust after her, put your eyes off and go your way".*

2. **MORTIFICATION:** *"Mortify, therefore, your members which are upon the earth, fornication, uncleanness",* etc. (Colossians 3:5-10, Romans 8:13. 2). To mortify is to bring about the death of a portion of a live body. Some items must be eliminated in another way since we cannot amputate them. Weak nerves, impatience, pride, and other such traits are among the problems in our lives that will require time to overcome. These need to be eliminated via mortification, and this should be internal rather than external. This procedure is more "medical" than "surgical." We must allow God to "operate in us," rather than exerting our own will (Philippians 2:12-13).

3. **LIMITATION:** *"Lay aside every weight, and the sin which doth so easily beset us"* (Hebrews 12:1. 3). There are two types of 'sins and weights': though all 'sins' are 'weights', not all 'weights' are 'sins'. Being devoted to your work or business is not wrong, but being so

preoccupied with doing good deeds that you overlook other vital tasks is 'weight' and should be kept to a minimum because they hinder the normal development of your spiritual life. On the other hand, every sin is a 'weight' since it makes it harder for us to run the Christian race and weighs us down.

Conclusion: *We gladden God's heart when we worship Him appropriately. He meets with us and restores unto us His image and likeness, which we lost as a result of sin. He does this to promote, encourage, and facilitate holy and continuous fellowship between us and Him.*

QUESTIONS

1. Expatiate on 'Spirit' and 'Truth' for worship.
2. Explain how worship requires the Truth of men as approved by the 'truth of God.'
3. What can you do with respect to Divine worship?

Notes

Study Fifteen

APPROPRIATE WORSHIP (PART 4)

MEMORY VERSE: *"See that you make them according to the pattern shown you on the mountain"* (Exodus 25:40).

BIBLE PASSAGE: Exodus 40:1-38.

INTRODUCTION

Jesus Christ is the tabernacle of meeting where man and his Creator are reconciled (Exodus 33:7-11, 2 Corinthians 5:18-21, Ephesians 2:11-22, Colossians 1:15-23). He is the foundation upon which all worship is built. He is God's Truth through whom our worship is admired and approved of God. He is the dividing line between religion and worship. The Bible says, *"Yet a time is coming and has come now when the true worshippers will worship the Father in Spirit (Holy Spirit) and truth (Jesus Christ), for they are the kind of worshippers the father seeks"* (John 4:23).

The expression "...is coming" indicates that there was never a time before Jesus Christ when the Father was truly worshipped, and "has come now" indicates that His arrival has brought us into true worship. For our worship to be appropriate, Father must be worshipped in Jesus Christ as well as through Jesus Christ. That, notwithstanding, some people recognize the 'Truth' but refuse to worship God in Him. They are like fatherless children. The Holy Spirit is the Father, while the Truth is Jesus, the word, and the mother. These people claim to believe Jesus is God's messenger, some even believe and quote scriptures from the beginning to the end, but the Holy Spirit is not in them. Jesus said, *"...And I will ask the Father, and he will give another counsellor to be with you forever. The Spirit of Truth (the Spirit of Christ), the world cannot accept Him because it neither sees Him nor knows Him. But you know Him, for He lives with you and will be in you. I will not leave you as orphans, I will come to you."* (John 14:16-18).

The 'Spirit' and the 'truth' must come together to form a union before your worship can be approved of God.

Outline:

Worship in the Tabernacle Pattern

WORSHIP IN THE TABERNACLE PATTERN

The tabernacle was God's design for Moses for worship. It was not a new invention because it was fashioned after the abode of Yahweh in heaven, where the angelic bodies worship (Revelation 4:1-11, Revelation 15:5, Exodus 25:40)

God's primary purpose for the tabernacle among men was to replicate and extend worship beyond the angelic world, meaning worship did not start with men. It was the full practice of the angelic bodies before even the foundation of the world. So, it has a pattern created for it which not even the angels can utter. Can you now see why you cannot worship God in your own unique way but God's own way?

Orthodox or true worship must follow the pattern of the tabernacle as given to Moses and fulfilled in Christ. The tabernacle has three segments: **The Gate**, which comprises the courtyard and the Altar of Sacrifice, **The Holy Place**, where there are: Table of Show-bread, Golden lamp stand, and Golden Altar of incense, Lastly, **The Holy of Holies**, where you can find the Ark of Testimony, inside of which are a pot of manna, tablets of the law and Aaron's rod. Now, to prove Himself as the fulfilment of the tabernacle, Christ said, "I am the WAY, the TRUTH and the LIFE. No one comes to the Father except through me" (John 14:6).

1. **The Gate:** This speaks of the ministry of Jesus Christ as the only **WAY** that leads to the Ark (GOD). It has a courtyard where we can find the brazen altar of sacrifice, which denotes Jesus as our sacrifice. His body was set on fire by the Holy Spirit on the cross of life. It represents Christ as the foundation of life (Lev 17: 11, 1 Corinthians 3: 10-12). Just as there was no gate, no other brazen altar, except the one provided at the outer space of the tabernacle, so also, there is no other way to true worship, except through Jesus Christ, the sacrificial Lamb of God for the human world (John 1: 29).

APPROACH

To approach or worship at the level of the gate, you need to:

- Accept Jesus Christ as your personal Lord and Saviour,
- Believe in His death substitute and that through Him only, you can reach God,
- Deny self-will to embrace God's will,
- Live a life cultivated for praise and thanksgiving in all situations (1Thessalonians 5: 16- 18, Psalms 100).

2. **The Holy Place:** contained in this segment of the tabernacle are (i) Table of show-bread, which speaks the divine **TRUTH**, and which is the strength of God to set believers free (John 8: 32), and life to whosoever finds it. Jesus is the word of God which is empowered by the Holy Spirit for divine service (John 1:14, 32). (ii) Golden lamp stand: this is the only light in the tabernacle, pointing to Jesus Christ as the only light of the world (John 9:5). It speaks of the Truth of God's word for liberation and righteousness. (Psalms 119: 105, Matthew 5:1 16). (iii) Golden Altar of Incense: is the divine Truth pointing to Jesus as the mediator and intercessor. It explains the praying heart of Jesus Christ in and for believers.

APPROACH

To worship God at this level:

- You must have accomplished the first segment,
- Have the right knowledge of the God you serve through His word (Bible),
- Make your body the abode of the Holy Spirit and where the fire of God must ever be present, (Revelation 12: 182 Corinthians 6:19-20, 2 Corinthians 6: 16).
- Develop personal devotion through the daily study of the Bible and having a heart of prayer to make communication with God possible,

3. **The Holy of Holies:** Here, you find **The Ark** contains (i) a Pot of manna, which typifies the word as the strength of God to walk with Him in the journey of life, (ii) The tablets of the law are the rules guiding true worship and facilitates self-discipline to be qualified for heavenly citizenship, (iii) The Rod of Aaron: these points to the guide or support to walk with God in His direction. **The Ark** speaks of Jesus Christ as the eternal **LIFE** and our meeting place with God. It is our

shield and safety. Through Jesus Christ in our life, God can dwell in us as His Temple.

APPROACH

This last segment is the level at which you speak with God as Moses did: Mouth-to-mouth and eyes-to-eyes (Exodus 33: 11a). To worship at this stage:

- You must have fulfilled the first and second segments,
- Worship in the way of the angels i.e. with all humility, seriousness and discipline (Revelation 4:8-11).

Conclusion: *Our God is Love, as well as God of discipline. Through discipline, His love becomes meaningful and perfect. Therefore, no relationship exists without discipline, and that is why worship must be done appropriately.*

QUESTIONS

1. Relate the items in the tabernacle to Jesus Christ as the only WAY to true worship.
2. How do you intend to appropriate worship from today?

Notes

Study Sixteen

APPROPRIATE WORSHIP (PART 5)

MEMORY VERSE: *"Rooted and build up in him, strengthened in the faith as you were taught, and overflowing with thanksgiving"* (Colossians 2:7).

BIBLE PASSAGE: Ephesians 3:14-21

INTRODUCTION

Once upon a time, in the midst of a discussion with a Christian believer and a drunk who could not speak a word without backing it up with the Scriptures, I said, *"Do not be filled with wine, be filled with the Holy Spirit"* (Ephesians 5:18). His response gave me a shocker, "Must everyone become a Pastor? Why must I be filled with the Holy Spirit?"

So many believers are like that. They believe and follow Jesus Christ but do not see any reason why they should solidify their relationship with Him, just as others do.

Outlines:

The Five Circles of Christians

The Five Circles of Christians

The following five circles are positions of people to Christ and worship in the Church.

First Circle "The Five Hundred" (Circle of Faith)

"After that, He was seen of above five hundred brethren at once, of whom the greater part remains unto this present, but some are fallen asleep." (1 Corinthians 15:6 (KJV))

The first circle is the circle of believers who have faith in Jesus Christ, and are saved, but see no reason why they should walk in nearness to

Him or become more active in the faith of Christ. They attend virtually all church programmes, but find no need to become committed other than being a 'bench warmer'. "After all, I don't like to be a Pastor," so they say. In their own belief, Pastors need God more than the members because, "they are in the position to pray for us, not we praying for ourselves or others". The Holy Spirit fullness is to them of no use if only they can have Pastors around. They follow Christ from afar and have no commitment other than, "Pastor, pray for me, Come to my house for the vigil, etc."

Second Circle "Circle of Seventy" (Circle of service)

"After these things, the Lord appointed other 'seventy' also, and sent them two and two before His face into every city and place, whither He Himself would come. Therefore, said He unto them, the harvest truly is great, but the labourers are few: pray ye, therefore, to the Lord of the harvest that, He would send forth labourers into His harvest. Go your ways. Behold, I send you forth as lambs among wolves." (Luke 10:1-11 (KJV)).

Out of the numerous followers of Christ, only seventy were available for service. He sent them "two and two" and gave instructions as to their conduct, where to go, what to do and what to say. They became His representatives and shared in His power to reach out and minister to those areas or people He was not likely to physically reach. They said, "Even the devil subjected to us through the name of Jesus Christ" (Luke 10: 17). In this circle today, we have only a few, in proportion to membership of our churches, which are available and fit for service. They can afford to work but with a 50% commitment. They spend the available rest time on secular work, parties, friends and other pleasurable things. They are always in haste and cannot wait for too long in the Church because they have other personal businesses, often time, to attend to. Immediately after discharging their duties for the day, they don't re-surface until another worship day. No robbing minds with the Pastor on ways to develop the Church, no time for evangelism, visitation, and sometimes, no time for weekly services.

Third Circle "Circle of Twelve" (Circle of Fellowship)

Among those who went farther with Christ were the two disciples. They were ordained by Christ to be with Him, to learn from Him and perform the same work He was doing to save the lost souls.

"And he goeth up into a mountain, and calleth unto him whom he would: and they came unto him. And he ordained twelve that they should be with him and that he might send them forth to preach, and to have the power to heal sicknesses, and to cast out devils." (Power of Darkness, Mark 3: 13-15 (KJV)). This is the category of people who have sincerely forsaken all so that they may gain Christ. They want to be known by Christ, fellowship with Him always and are eager to reach out and fulfil the task of Evangelism.

Fourth Circle "The Circle of the Three" (The Circle of Privilege)

Jesus Christ chooses among the twelve, three men to go with Him on special occasions. Those men were Peter, James, and John. They were called out of the twelve disciples for untold reasons. However, unknown to them, they had special work ahead of them. Peter was to lead the Apostles, James was to be the Head of the Church in Jerusalem, and John was to be the 'Apocalyptic seer' of the Church. To fulfil these special tasks, it becomes imperative that the three agree and never question the DEITY of Jesus Christ. Owing to this, Jesus took them to places where His DEITY could be manifest to them. The three were with Jesus at the home of Jairus (Mark 5:2243); where He revealed His resurrection power, the Mount of Transfiguration; where He revealed His glory (Mark 9:1-10), the Garden of Gethsemane; where he revealed His SORROW, that they might have the vision of what the suffering of the cross cost Him. It was a great privilege for these three to behold the revelation of Christ's POWER, GLORY and SUFFERING.

Today, we have a few people who have got the privilege of moving very closely with Christ and their Pastor to share with Him the Power, Glory and Sufferings of His ministry, which are unknown to the world and yet, increase their faith.

Fifth Circle "Circle of One (Circle of Love)

It is possible you are in the circle of three and not in the circle of one because it envisages love with passion.

Jesus said, *"A new commandment I give you. That ye love one another, as I have LOVED you, that ye may also LOVE one another. By this shall all men know that ye are my Disciples if ye have love one another"* (John 13:34, 35).

Among Christ's disciples, only John was able to fulfil the commandment to 'love one another' exceptionally and so, was loved by Jesus Christ: *"...the disciples whom Jesus loved"* (John 21:20).

The proof of his love for Christ and one another was seen in the wonderful fourth chapter of his first Epistle, where he used the word 'love' 26 times. Moreover, on the arrest of Jesus, when all other disciples forsook the Lord and fled, Peter, denied knowing Him. John was the only exception who went with Jesus to the High Priest, where He was tried (John 18:5). Likewise, in our churches, there are very few men who love Christ by obeying His commandments. They will never sin nor deny ever knowing Christ, no matter the odds. They move closely with Him and can hear Him when He speaks. They cherish personal worship as well as public worship. They never thought of what Christ or the Church could do for them but what they could do for Christ and the Church.

Conclusion: *Having learned about these circles, to which do you belong? Christianity is a life in stages. Do you ever bother to move to the next stage? Let today's lesson be an opportunity for you to move to circle one, where you can speak mouth-to-mouth, face-to-face with the Lord our God.*

QUESTIONS

1. How best can you solidify your relationship with Christ?
2. List ten steps to be taken in order to join circle one.
3. How do you intend to assist your Pastor in the work of ministry?

Notes

Study Seventeen

WHAT CHRISTIANITY IS NOT

MEMORY VERSE: *"For the kingdom of God is not a matter of talk but power"* (1 Corinthians 4: 20).

BIBLE PASSAGES: Mark 9: 38-40, Mark 7:15-23

INTRODUCTION

In Mark 9: 38-40, a report came to Jesus that a man was driving out demons in Christ's name. According to John, "...and we told him to stop because HE WAS NOT ONE OF US." Jesus responded, *"Do not stop him, No one does miracles in my name and in the next moment say anything bad about me, for whoever is not against us is for us."*

In contrast to the afore-said, in Matt. 7:22, Christ said, *"Many will say to me on that day, 'Lord, Lord, did we not prophesy in YOUR NAME and in YOUR NAME drive out demons and performed many miracles? Then I will tell them plainly that I never knew you. Go away from me, you evildoers!"* There are two lessons to be learned from these two quotations: Using Christ's name and Living Christ-like.

Outlines:

1. Using Christ's name
2. Living Christ-like

USING CHRIST'S NAME:

The point of similarity and dissimilarity between these two groups is the fact that they both drove out the devil in Christ's name but were not enlisted among Christ's disciples. The first was not known to the disciples (Mark. 9:38), and the second was not known to Christ (Matt.7:22, 23).

UNKNOWN TO THE DISCIPLES: This is the category of people we call unbelievers because we think they are not with us in our churches. They are not enlightened in the word of God, they are not dressed in our "dress code" but are Christians in the heart. They believe in Jesus and call on His name even when they cannot openly confess Him because of persecution and penalties inflicted for doing so under the laws guiding the land or the community. Examples of such people are in Saudi Arabia, Afghanistan, China, and other Arabian continents. Christ understands their predicaments and honours His name in their mouths. He said, "...whosoever is not against us is for us".

UNKNOWN TO CHRIST: This category of people, either in freedom or bondage, has chosen to only have Christ's name in their mouth and not in their heart. Christ honours His name sometimes, not because the caller is honourable but because the name is above all names and that God may be glorified (Philippians 2:9-11).

Just as we turn our necks towards the direction where our name is called, whether the caller is known or not, Christ likewise responds to people when they call His name. He might decide to be generous to the caller, but not because the caller is known to Him. He said, "Not everyone who says to me, 'Lord, Lord will enter the Kingdom of Heaven, but only he who does the will of my father who is in heaven" (Matt. 7:21).

LIVING CHRIST-LIKE: The second lesson that could be learned from the two quotations is LIVING CHRIST-LIKE. Calling Christ's name ends here, but living Christ-like goes beyond earthly stay (Matt. 7:21, Philippians 2:5). Living Christ-like is the same as doing the father's will. Whomever you may be, if you are not doing the will of God, you are not known to Christ, as far as, He is concerned. You are not known to Him simply means your name is not written in the book of life. That is, even though you call unto His name on earth, if His will is not done, the end will become a disaster, discomfort and agony in hellfire.

Conclusion: *We are reaching towards knowing who a Christian is. It is not all the people you call infidels are indeed infidels, and it is not all the people you call Christians that are Christians indeed.*

Questions:

1. How can you identify a true Christian?
2. What can you do to become one?

Notes

Study Eighteen

WHAT CHRISTIANITY IS NOT (PART 2)

MEMORY VERSE: "For the Kingdom of God is not a matter of eating and drinking, but of righteousness, peace and joy in the Holy Spirit" (Romans 14:17).

BIBLE PASSAGES: Mark 7:1-23, Mark 8:34 – 38.

INTRODUCTION "A Christian is someone who goes to church, pays his tithe, reads his bible, calls on God, evangelizes and performs Christian rites." Is that not what your definition of a Christian is? Christianity is life, it goes beyond mere Christian rites. It is the love you reveal by dying to your self-will only for His (God's) will to be done. It is a life lived in process of becoming as He (Christ) is.

Outlines:

1. What Christianity is not?
2. What is Christianity?

WHAT CHRISTIANITY IS NOT

Let it be clear to us that Christianity is not:

1. Observing the laws of God,
2. Being well-educated in the word of God,
3. Occupying a position in the Church,
4. Commitment to church activities,
5. Being self-righteous,
6. Merely full of good works,
7. Giving alms or donations,
8. Evangelizing,
9. Dressing Christian way,
10. Choosing it (Christianity) as a religious choice,
11. Founding of churches or being eloquent as a preacher,
12. Exercising spiritual gifts,

13. Identifying with Christians or boasting of the Pastors you know,
14. Reading the Bible cover-to-cover,
15. Emulating Christian saints, etc.

However, all these are expected of you if you have become a Christian.

WHAT CHRISTIANITY IS

It is:

1. Accepting the Grace of God,
2. Having Christ implanted in you,
3. Showing love to God and humans,
4. Dying to self to live in Christ,
5. Shining as God's light in the darkness of life (i.e. living a life different from sinners),
6. Having endless enmity with Satan and his cohorts,
7. Having your will in submission to fulfil Christ's will,
8. A life is not lived alone but in communion with the Holy Spirit,
9. A total reliance on the Creator alone,
10. A life living towards being like Christ,
11. Having the same mind as God and his saints,
12. Doing the same judgement with God (i.e. hating what he hates and loving what he loves),
13. Living with the consciousness of imminent rapture and the choice of heaven,
14. Righteousness with earthly relevance,
15. A real life not in pretence,
16. A life continuously burning of the revival fire of the Holy Ghost, etc.

Conclusion: Having said these, judge yourself, Are you a Christian? If No is your answer, then start doing something about it now? Our purpose in being Christians is to be like Christ.

QUESTIONS

1. What other characteristics of a Christian can you think of?
2. Can a man be saved by merely having good work? Discuss.

Notes

Study Nineteen

WHAT DOES CHRIST EXPECT FROM YOU?

MEMORY VERSE: "So you also, when you have done everything you were told to do, should say, we are unworthy servants. We have only done our duty" (Luke 17:10).

BIBLE PASSAGE: Luke 17:1 – 10

INTRODUCTION

Now that you are a Christian, what does Christ expect from you? In any organization, every member is expected to perform a certain function to retain his/her membership. Suppose you signed up to be a member of an organization and enjoyed its privileges but refused to perform the duties expected of you. What happens to your membership? Membership in any organization has some privileges as well as responsibilities.

In Christianity, we have Christ as our Head, the foundation of every true Church. The blessing we enjoy from Him being the Head and the foundation of the Church cannot be numbered, and the fact that some of these blessings are not without responsibilities is not an overstatement.

In today's study, we shall consider four responsibilities that Jesus taught His followers to fulfil.

Outline:

Four Things Christ Expects from you as a Christian

FOUR THINGS CHRIST EXPECTS FROM YOU AS A CHRISTIAN

The four responsibilities Christ expects from you are stated as follows:

1. To Remove Stumbling Blocks

"Jesus said to his disciples: Things that cause people to sin are bound to come, but woe to that person through whom they come. It would be better for him to be thrown into the sea with a millstone tied around his neck than for him to cause one of these little ones to sin. So take heed to yourselves" (Luke 17:1 - 3a).

The man who murders life is not the most dangerous, but the man who murders soul by teaching false doctrines that may lead to eternal damnation. Recognizing this fact, Jesus warned His disciples of the possibility of the arrival of false teachers who, through deception, would cause people to lose their salvation and, as a result, their eternal home. Christ, in order to further express His dissatisfaction with this likelihood, advised what should preferably be done to those who behave in this manner, saying that a milestone should be tied around their neck and cast into the sea. On the other hand, this refers to the severity of the punishment they will inevitably get in the afterlife.

Our responsibility, therefore, is to keep watch and warn people of God against such preachers. Never to overlook heresies but to rebuke them sharply using the undiluted word of God.

2. Forgiveness

"If your brother sins, rebuke him, and if he repents, forgive him. If he sins against you seven times in a day, and seven times comes back to you and says, "I repent', forgive him" (Luke 17:3b – 4).

Christianity differs from other religious groups in that it is known for its simplicity in forgiving sin. This is due to the fact that Jesus said that forgiveness was a requirement for divine pardon for the sins that may have caused us to spend all eternity in hellfire (Matthew 6: 14, 15). That is, if we provide forgiveness to those who have harmed us, God will do likewise and pardon us for our sins (1. John 1:9). Forgiveness does not mean to ignore offences, it is to draw offenders' attention to the issues that led to the grievances for correction. It is addressing issues while releasing personalities involved from the depths of our minds as if nothing had been done through them. As Christians, our responsibility is not to condemn anyone because God loves sinners as well so that they may come to know the Truth. We are to forgive those who have wronged us for the simple reason that they may come to know the Truth through forgiveness. Furthermore, we are to preach forgiveness when our own forgiveness is complete (2 Corinthians 10:6).

3. Faith Like A Mustard Seeds

The apostles said to the Lord, "Increase our faith". He (Jesus) replied, if you have faith as small as a mustard seed, you can say to this mulberry tree, 'Be uprooted and planted in the sea,' and it will obey you" (Luke 17:56).

We cannot undermine what depravity has caused humankind. It has robbed us of exercising our faith and made virtually everything absolutely unrealizable. Nonetheless, Jesus taught believers that even the most difficult tasks require only a little faith to complete.

Indeed, my years in ministry taught me that even the highest mountain in the world requires only a leap of faith to reach the sea. Jesus' teaching did not prepare us to be fearful soldiers. As God incarnates on earth, we are to boldly speak the unseen into the apparent, and it is expected of us to make things either in or out of us happen by the assurance that our God is capable of doing anything if we ask Him (Luke 1:37, Matthew 19:26).

4. Dutiful Obedience

"Suppose one of you had a servant ploughing or looking after the sheep, would he say to the servant when he comes in from the field, 'Come along now and sit down to eat'? Would he not rather say, "Prepare my supper, get yourself ready and wait on me while I eat and drink. After that, you may eat and drink?' Would he thank the servant because he did what he was told to do? So you also, when you have done everything you were told to do, should say, 'We are unworthy servants, we have only done our duty" (Luke 17:7-10).

"Thank God we're all Christians, but why do you think you need God personally?" I asked in our Bible study meeting a few years ago.

(Please, teacher, direct this question to each of your students, and then proceed with your study.)

Are these their reactions: because of Heaven, blessings, miracles, staying alive, and so on? If so, they are consistent with the responses I've received from others. However, if I am to respond to the question, I will say that I do not serve God because of all of those reasons. I serve Him and will continue to serve Him because I love Him more than what words can express. When something goes beyond mere words, it shows in your actions and reactions. As Christians, we must stop working for Him because of the benefits or rewards we will receive from Him. Because we love Him, we are expected to carry out our Christian responsibilities.

When it comes to love, Jesus said that if we claim to love Him, we should follow his instructions (John 14:15). As a result, we should not love or serve Him because of the rewards we will receive from Him but, rather, because we love Him.

Sometimes during a job interview, the interviewer asked me, "Why do you want to work with us?" I was perplexed for few seconds before I could respond to him. My confusion was, "Should I say because I needed money or because I needed a job?" Then, I realised those might not be the expected answers, and in response, I said, "I love what I know, and I'm able to do. I also love to do what I know how to do best in your company which I so much love." This, I believe, was a very good response because you cannot love me for what you can get from me. That isn't love (John 6: 25-29, 21: 15 – 17).

Our Christian service does not place any obligation on our master. Jesus illustrated this in verse 10 of today's text. Public thanks and recognition of Christian service should not be expected. I often say, and it has become my slogan whenever I place my request before God, "If you do it, Sir, then you are my God, and if you don't, then you will continue to be my God." I think we should see Christian service just like that. God does not owe us anything, we are only doing our duties as unworthy servants. We should not give to Him for His blessings in return. Rather, we should give because we love Him and His work to continue. He may choose to bless us in return, but He owns no allegiance to us as far as our Christian service is concerned. Does this mean we should not hope in His glory and blessings? No! Since His love attracts glory and rewards to us, seek his love first (Matthew 6:33, John 14:21).

It is expected of us, therefore, to dutifully obey His instructions concerning our Christian service, not with eye service or having hope only in the rewards. His love is absolutely rewarding, His work is just as slaves do the work of their masters, not minding the rewards (Colossians 22:25).

Conclusion: "I died. I died because of you. What have you done for me? (Check the Baptist Hymn)". After making every effort to save us from the pangs of death and Hell, Christ now demands that we fulfil our obligations and never leave our covenant with Him unfulfilled.

QUESTIONS

1. What does it mean "to leave our covenant with Him unfulfilled?"
2. What other things do you think Christ expects from us as Christians?

Notes

Study Twenty

A WINNING CHRISTIAN LIFE

MEMORY VERSE: "What is more, I consider everything a loss compared to the surpassing greatness of knowing Christ Jesus my Lord, for whose sake I have lost all things. I considered them rubbish that I may gain Christ" (Philippians 3: 8)

BIBLE PASSAGE: Ephesians 6:12a, 2Corinthians 10:3-6, Philippians 3: 1-16

INTRODUCTION:

When a spiritual battle breaks out, some people do not see reasons for fighting. To reach an amicable resolution, they choose to appease 'the elders' or the gods. Appeasing your enemies implies that you have agreed that they are the winner and you are the loser, even when there was no struggle. It means you've given up control of your life and possessions to them, and you're happy with whatever they do with them. It means you've abandoned your life mission, which is the source of the conflict. It means you agree with your adversaries' analysis of the conditions for peace: have some and lose some. Even if it makes you more of God's enemy, as long as you are allowed to accomplish certain things that your enemies approve of, you are at peace.

I'll never be able to make peace with my spiritual adversaries. It is a battle to the finish, and I am the victor because I am not fighting alone. The Lord of Hosts is by my side. In a battle, a fully armed soldier does not seek to appease his opponents, otherwise, he will become a prey. As Christians, we must fight and win.

Outlines:

1. Reasons why you must fight.
2. Why you must win?

REASONS WHY YOU MUST FIGHT

Our spiritual foes are always prepared to fight. If you are unwilling to fight, then they will still fight even if you believe you have not offended them. You don't have to offend them physically before they declare war on you. Their annoyance is justified by your existence and God's assignment. Therefore, you must fight for the following reasons:

- They want to manipulate, intimidate, and finally dominate your life,
- They want to destroy and therefore are fighting to hinder your glory, peace, and good health so that you don't become a terror to their kingdom,
- They are fighting to make you an enemy of God and, thereafter, make you live forever in Hell, their final destination,
- They want to make your life miserable and make you regret ever coming to this earth,
- Once they achieve all these, they want to cut-short your life's span so that you don't regain what is lost.

WHY YOU MUST WIN

Winning our spiritual battle is of necessity because:

- ❖ Our soul and that of others are at stake. We need to win to save our souls and that of others in order to become heavenly citizens,
- ❖ We need to win to enjoy all that God has predetermined for our beautiful stay here on earth,
- ❖ We must win to finish strong and have good rewards at the end of our earthly struggle because there is no reward for work half-done,
- ❖ God expects nothing other than winning because weapons of war are already given, and they must not return to God without the stain of our enemies' blood splattered all over them,
- ❖ Heaven celebrates winners,

Conclusion: Let us all know that 'winners don't quit and quitters don't win.' 'It is not the end until you win' said Pastor Ashimolowo. Only the cowards fright at hearing the sound of war. Therefore, let us fight the spiritual battle, for our Lord is with us to guarantee victory (I Tim 6:12).

QUESTIONS

1. Are you encountering a spiritual battle presently? How do you aim at winning?
2. Highlight three spiritual weapons you intend to use in the battle.

Notes

Study Twenty-One

OUR INSTRUMENTS OF WAR

MEMORY VERSE: *"Put on the full Armour of God so that you can take your stand against the devil's schemes" (Ephesians 6:11)*

BIBLE PASSAGE: *Ephesians 6:10-20, 2 Corinthians 10:3-4*

INTRODUCTION

A spiritual military operation has all in common with terrestrial military activities. Starting from the discipline, strenuous training, defensive and offensive operations and military services altogether. The only marked contrast is the fact that while one operates in the physical and has human soldiers as its commanders, the other is spiritual and has our Lord Jesus Christ as its eternal and seven-star General Commander. On account of this, war preparation, weapons, and fighting methods are all incompatible. However, the two types of war instruments—defensive and offensive—remain common. If one is ever absent, the soldier is nothing more than a prey to the enemies.

Going to battle without adequate war instruments is a sign of loss before the battle begins.

Outlines:

1. Four Steps to overcoming life
2. Defensive and offensive strategies
3. Attitudes to war
4. The result of overcoming war

Four Steps to Overcoming Life

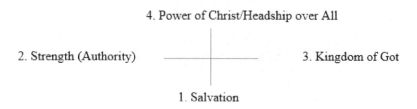

4. Power of Christ/Headship over All

2. Strength (Authority)   3. Kingdom of Got

1. Salvation

SALVATION:

The first step to a winning Christian life is salvation. Without it, you cannot embark on any spiritual battle because a life not saved is sinful, and a sinful life is already a prey to the devil. Salvation is God's way of preserving us from trouble or danger, delivering us from sin and its consequences and implanting His life in us in order to fight on our behalf. Left to us, we are powerless, but through Him, we can do all things (John 5:4, 5, Philippians. 4:13). To be saved, therefore, you need genuine repentance and a heart completely turned and washed in the blood of Jesus Christ.

STRENGTH (AUTHORITY):

This is defined as power or dignity, a warrant or order (Matthew 7:29, Luke 10:17 21:23, Acts 9:14). However, for clarity, I will say, Authority is the right to speak on God's behalf. When Christ saves, the person saved is given the authority to speak on Christ's behalf at any time. This is our ability and strength to live a triumphant life. The authority of Christ, which is our strength, can be obtained only through His word and name (Mark. 16:17, John 14 John 2:14b, Numbers 22:38).

KINGDOM OF GOD:

The kingdom of God is the spiritual territory, rule, control, and protection of God. It is the kingdom opposed to by the devil because it is the stronghold of God, where the children of God are trained, equipped and empowered to depopulate and absolutely desolate the kingdom of darkness. You cannot face the spiritual enemy in battle if you are not in God's kingdom. To be in His kingdom, you must submit your life and will to God in Christ (Romans 12, James 4:7).

POWER OF CHRIST / HEADSHIP OVER ALL:

As Commander in Chief, He leads us to the battleground. He is our strength, through which we can live a victorious life. Our own strength is insufficient to engage in a Christian battle. But through His power, we have the strength to fight (Acts 1:8, Phi. 4:13). When we reach the point where Christ's power becomes our power, and His headship draws our submission, we become a terror to the satanic kingdom.

Our **Defensive** and **Offensive** strategies for a winning Christian life (Ephesians 6:10-17).

DEFENSIVE	OFFENSIVE
Truth:	Sword of the Spirit (Word of God)
Righteousness:	The blood of Jesus Christ (Revelation 13:8)
Peace:	The name of Jesus Christ (Mark. 16:17; Philippians 1:2, 9, 10)
Salvation:	The power of Jesus Christ (Matt 28:18; Matt. 10:1; Luke. 4:33, 36)

Key Note: These weapons can effectively be used through prayer, fasting and a life of holiness. Otherwise, the offensive weapons can turn against the user (Ephesians 6:18, Matthew 17:21, Mark. 9:29, Hebrews 12:14).

Attitudes to War

Man's attitude to war, in both physical and spiritual, is very important because it determines whether you will win or lose the battle. These attitudes include:

1. Willingness (2 Corinthians 8:12, Philemon 14, 1 Pet 5:2),
2. Discipline (Job 36:10),
3. Obedience (Exodus 23:22),
4. Consistency (Philippians. 6:13)
5. Striking: the best defence.

THE RESULT OF OVERCOMING LIFE

God will wipe away tears:

No more:

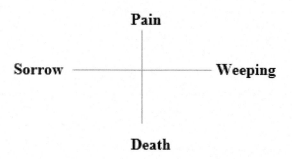

Pain

Sorrow ——————— Weeping

Death

Conclusion:

Our instruments of war are not carnal but strong, effective, reliable, and available to every believer in the Lord Jesus Christ.

QUESTIONS

1. List and explain how each of the Defensive and Offensive spiritual weapons can be put to use.
2. When last did you fight a spiritual battle? What was your experience like?

Notes

Study Twenty-Two

BAPTISM OF SUFFERING

MEMORY VERSE: "It is better if it is God's will to suffer for doing good than for doing evil" (1 Pet 3:17)

BIBLE PASSAGE: 1 Peter 3:8- 22, 1 Pet. 2:11, 12

INTRODUCTION

Preachers who say, "No more pain if you accept Jesus Christ," are heretic. I believe we should inform people that suffering is a necessary part of their newly accepted faith—not suffering as an evildoer who is being punished by God, but as a good witness and follower of Christ who has chosen to endure suffering in order to effectively carry out his mission on earth.

Early in the Church history, Satan made an attempt to douse the apostles' flame of faith, but in doing so, he accidentally spread the flame, which immediately conflagrated and spread to all other nations in accordance with God's intention.

The enemies of faith may think you are being made to suffer, not knowing that the suffering is also to fulfil a purpose. Many believers know little about the baptism called "Baptism of Suffering". Holy Ghost and Water Baptisms are more popular to them. However, our Lord Jesus Christ talked of the three baptisms to significantly identify with his life and death. He talked of water baptism as an ordinance of the Church when He Himself was baptised (Matt. 4). He spoke of Holy Ghost baptism when He asked His disciples to wait for the promise of the Father (Acts. 1 & 2).

Finally, in His response to the request of James and John's mother to have her children sit, one on the right and one on the left, respectively, in His kingdom, Jesus said, "You don't know what you are asking"... "Can you drink the cup I drink or be baptised with the BAPTISM I am baptised with? "We can", they answered. Jesus said to them, "You will drink the cup I drink and be baptised with the baptism 1 am baptised with, but to sit at my right or left is not for me to grant" (Mar 10:38 – 39).

Jesus Christ here was not referring to water baptism because many people, even most of His disciples, had gone through the baptism of John the Baptist. He could not have asked the question, "Can you?" if it were to be Holy Ghost baptism since He was still going to beg the Father for the promise. He meant the 'cup of death' and the 'Baptism of suffering' which years later, John and James were baptised with (Acts 12:10 2, Revelation 1:9, Matt. 26" 36 - 46)

Outlines:

1. What is baptism of suffering?
2. Suffering for self or Christ?
3. Rewards for suffering for Christ

WHAT IS BAPTISM OF SUFFERING?

Baptism is from the Greek word, 'baptizo' meaning to 'immerse or deep in' and 'suffering' means to endure pain or anguish. Since in water baptism, we say to 'immerse in water', and in Holy Ghost baptism, we say to 'immerse in the Holy Ghost', so also, is the 'Baptism of suffering', which means to immerse, deep or have one's wish in the endurance of pain and anguish for the sake of the gospel of Christ (Acts 17:20, 2 Corinthians 6:3-13, 2Corinthians 11:21-33). Peter added, "If you suffer, it should not be as a murderer or thief or any other kind of criminal or even as a meddler. However, if you suffer as a Christian, do not be ashamed, but praise God that you bear that name" (1 Peter. 4:15-16).

No one prays for suffering, but as Christians, suffering must not seem to us as outrageous. It is part of Christianity. Christ said, "Whoever is willing to follow Him must bear his / her cross" (Matt. 10:37, 39). This means whosoever is willing to be Christ's follower must deny his/her 'I and my syndrome', which is 'self', and be ready to encounter or endure whatever anguish is placed on our Christian journey as a trial of faith. Suffering may take different routes, which could include: financial hardship, ill health, persecution, or even death, for the gospel's sake. Whichever way it takes in your life, know this "weeping may endure for a night, but joy comes in the morning" (Psalms 30:5b, Romans 8:18, 1 Pet. 3:1-22).

SUFFERING FOR SELF OR CHRIST?

As I was working on this study, I received this text message from a friend, "please pray for the 22 Christian Missionary Families that will be executed by Islamists today in Afghanistan. Please spread as fast and to as many as will pray."

Though it is a shocking, pathetic, and painful occurrence, but looking at the rewards set before people who suffer for the course of Christ, we can say that to die is gain (Philippians 1:20, 21). Christians are not to kill or respond by killing (Exodus 20: 13), the apostles did not kill despite the persecutions. On the contrary, Christians are trained by our Lord and Master Jesus Christ to die for the faith. Jesus Christ had the power to resist the cross, but "for the sake of the joy set before Him, He endured the shame and pains of the cross" (Hebrews 12:2b, John 18:1-6). We must not suffer for the sake of our evil desires, wrongdoings, unnecessary stubbornness, or disobedience (1 Pet. 2:11, 12), but we were commanded, if we must suffer, to suffer for Christ.

❖ **Suffering for Christ must be done with a ready mind (Philemon 14, II Corinthians 8:19b, James 1:8)**

When confronted with anguish, we must not be taken by surprise. It is what we automatically agree to when we accept to live like Christ (John 16:33).

❖ **Suffering for Christ must solely be based on Christ (Matt. 5:11, Matt. 10:22, 24:9**

No man should suffer for the sake of another. To be a faithful follower of Christ, each person must bear his or her own cross. Your suffering must not be motivated by what you stand to gain from man. It must not be motivated by ignorance, stubbornness, or greed. For example, establishing or organizing a church crusade in a government-forbidden area or disobeying local laws. If you do these things, you will suffer as a result of your arrogance and stubbornness (Romans 13: 1- 7). Rather than rebelling against such rules, pray for them to come to know the Truth (1 Timothy 2: 1-2).

❖ Suffering for Christ must be in Truth

The word of God is the Truth of Christ (John 14:6). Don't suffer for things that Christ did not command you to accomplish, but if you suffer in accordance with His commands and wills, you will experience peace in the end (John 16:33).

❖ Suffering for Christ must be with a joyful heart (John 15:33)

When Peter and John were beaten and threatened not to talk about Christ any longer, they counted it as joy to partake in Christ's suffering (Acts 4:21, 5:17 - 42). They did not feel sad or regret ever knowing Christ. Are you suffering for Christ right now? Count it all joy because it is not by force that you must suffer, not grudgingly, but willingly (2 Corinthians 9:7).

❖ Suffering for Christ must be with hope (Col 1:27b)

We have our hope in Christ's return and in the rewards and happiness hereafter. We do not suffer as one without hope (1 Thessalonians 4:13). When we suffer for Christ, we have the hope of having joy in Heaven as our reward.

❖ Suffering for Christ must focus on Christ (Hebrews 12:2)

Stephen, the first martyr, had his eyes fixed on Christ who was sitting at the right hand of God as he was being stoned by the criminals (Acts 7:54 - 60). In a similar manner, as we endure suffering for Christ's sake, we must keep our eyes fixed on Him because "Where your treasure is, there will also be your heart" (Matt. 6:21). It will be a wonderful relief when the emphasis is on Christ rather than on oneself or the suffering (i.e. Christ will bear your pain and you will receive additional strength to continue). You will also feel as though you are not suffering alone. Focus on Christ instead of yourself because He is the one the world rejects and despises, not you (Matthew 3:18–21).

Conclusion:

It is not enough to bring the Ark into our life. You must also be willing to face whatever anguish stands your way on account of Christ. "Christ in us, the Hope of Glory!" (Colossians 1: 27b).

QUESTIONS

1. Explain briefly what it means to suffer for Christ.
2. Have you gone through the three types of baptism? Explain your experience in each.

Notes

Study Twenty-Three

COMMUNION WITH THE HOLY SPIRIT

MEMORY VERSE: "The grace of the Lord Jesus Christ, and the love of God, and the communion of the Holy Ghost, be with you all" (2 Corinthians 13:14).

BIBLE PASSAGES: John 14:15-18, 26, John 16:5-16.

INTRODUCTION

Communion, in some other versions of the Bible, is used as fellowship. It means communicating with, travelling together, living with, or transporting with. Communion with the Holy Spirit can be explained in line with the fellowship that exists between a husband and his wife. In Genesis 2:18, God said, "it is not good for a man to be alone. I will make a helper suitable for him." The purpose of this union is mainly for companionship, procreation, and sexual satisfaction (Genesis 2:24, 25, Genesis 1:28, 1 Corinthians.7:2-6). Being that as it may, it is absolutely impossible for a Christian to be without the Holy Spirit. The Holy Spirit is the seal of God to claims His ownership of any Christian believer. It is the first gift that comes immediately after a life is won to Jesus Christ. (Acts 1:8, Acts 10:1-end, Acts 8: 4-25). It is also a sign of acceptance into God's kingdom of saints and endorsement for Christian service (Acts 15:8, Acts 13:2). It is a means by which God purifies the heart of a sinful man (Acts 15:9).

Outlines:

1. Who is the Holy Spirit?
2. Purpose of the Holy Spirit?

Who is the Holy Spirit?

The English word 'who' is used in a question asking about a person's name, identity, or functions. Hence using it for the Holy Spirit indicates that a personality is being referred to here. The Holy Spirit is a living being. He has emotions and can feel (Romans 5:5). He understands our situations thoroughly and assists us in our areas of weakness. He speaks (Revelation 27), He prays for us (Romans 8:26), He teaches us (John 16:13), He comforts believers (Acts 9:31), He has His will for believers (1 Corinthians 12:11, Acts 16:6, 7), etc.

The Holy Spirit, though a person, cannot be seen physically because, despite being a person, He is also God and the third member of the Godhead (the Father, Son, and Holy Spirit). We are not advocating polytheism (the belief in more than one God). Christians believe in only one God (Duet. 6:4). This one and only God, however, manifests Himself in three distinct personalities (1 John 8(NKJV)).

The Holy Spirit is God, and the following are the proofs:

- ❖ The Bible itself calls the Holy Spirit God (Matt. 28:19),
- ❖ Peter, one of the Disciples of Christ, called him God (Acts 5:3-4),
- ❖ Holy Spirit was present at creation (Genesis 1:2 job 26:13),
- ❖ He raised the dead (Romans 1:4, 6:11), caused people to be born again (John 3:5-7), reproved the world of sin, righteousness and judgement (John 16:8), and cast out devils (Matt. 12:28),

The Holy Spirit shares the same attributes with God e.g.

- ❖ He is eternal, and only God can be eternal (Hebrews 9:14),
- ❖ He is omniscient (He knows all things) (1 Corinthians 2:10),
- ❖ He is Omnipotent (Powerful) (Luke 1:35),
- ❖ He is omnipresent (His presence is everywhere) (Psalms 139),

Purpose of the Holy Spirit

Although the Holy Spirit has many purposes, we will only look at three that are closely linked to marriage purposes.

Marriage	Holy Spirit
1. Companionship	1. Companionship
2. Procreation	2. Procreation :
3. Sexual Satisfaction	3. Convict the world of Immorality
(to put a stop to sin)	guilt in regards to unrighteousness
	and judgement

1. **Companionship:** "It is not good for a man to be alone; I will make for him a help mate," God said in Genesis 2:18. It means that God did not make anyone an outcast. Man requires constant fellowship with man in order not to respond to the unknown world (i.e. go insane) and to have a desirable stay here on earth. To meet the demands of nature, you must share with someone, communicate with someone, travel with someone, or live with someone. Similarly, because man is both natural and spiritual, a spiritual outcast is more worthless than tits on a boar hog. The ability to strictly follow God's will and complete the divine mission, which is unachievable in our natural state, distinguishes the spiritual man from the natural man. To be able to recognize spiritual things and live a 100% natural and 100% spiritual life, you, therefore, need a spiritual companion who can share, converse, travel, and live with you for all eternity.

2. **Procreation:** "Be fruitful and increase in number, fill the earth and subdue it. Rule over" (Genesis 2:8). Man must reproduce in order to carry out God's plan for creation, and this cannot happen without being joined in marriage to another person. According to the master plan, procreation is also necessary for our spiritual existence. To bear fruit, grow in number, dominate, and rule over the earth. We need spiritual marriage to fulfil these, not to the familiar spirit of the spirit husband or wife, but to the Holy Spirit. Our relationship with Him will produce the offspring that will establish our favour

with God. The Bible refers to these offsprings as the "fruits of the spirit" (Galatians 5:22, 23). Although God may take into account natural barrenness, He has no interest in spiritual barrenness.

3. **Sexual Satisfaction:** Aside from the reason for procreation, a man must satisfy his sexual desires with his own spouse in order to avoid being caught in immorality with another man's wife. So, it is to avoid sin against man and against God (1 Corinthians 7:2). The Holy Spirit's mission is to convict the world of sin (convict means to judge, rebuke, correct, improve, and promote), righteousness and judgement. In other words, the Holy Spirit is to guide us against any known or unknown sin and to make us walk in God's will (John 16:13, 14).

Conclusion: *Fellowship with the Holy Spirit is not for a particular set of people in the Church. You can do more than your Pastor by making yourself a companion of the Holy Spirit from now on.*

Question

1. What are the benefits of being a man full of the Holy Spirit?
2. Why did God's word warn us against being filled with wine in Ephesians 5:18?

Notes

Study Twenty-Four

COMMUNION WITH HOLY SPIRIT (PART2)

MEMORY VERSE: "And I will ask the Father, and he will give you another counsellor to be with you forever" (John 14:16).

BIBLE PASSAGES: Ephesians 1:13-14

INTRODUCTION

The Holy Spirit guards the Father's things and properties. This protection comes in the form of instruction, empowerment, and healing to fulfil the Father's desires. In our natural state, we cannot fully enjoy God's protection because He settles for nothing less than His Holiness. To be qualified for His Holiness, the Holy Spirit must purify and deter us from our sinful nature before transporting us to the presence of our God, who desires worship in Spirit and Truth. Except when you have already experienced the transportation in the Spirit to have a good relationship with God in His holiness, you have not yet become a Christian.

Outlines:

1. Christian with the Holy Spirit
2. What should our attitude be toward the Holy Spirit?

Christian with the Holy Spirit

No man is saved unless he is born of the word of God and the Holy Spirit (John 3:5). Once you are born again, the Holy Spirit will reside in you as the Comforter and will assist you in your infirmities (John 14:16, Romans 8:1& 2).

This is important because the Holy Spirit must:

- ✧ Bring holiness into our life (Romans 8:1&2),
- ✧ Teach us all things (John 14:26),
- ✧ Lead us until we become sons of God (Romans 8:14),

- ✧ Be with us as a Comforter in times of sorrow (John 14:16, 18),
- ✧ Confirm in us that we are God's children (Galatians 4:6),
- ✧ Empower us for divine services (Acts 1:8), and
- ✧ thereafter, take us to heaven. People without the Holy Spirit are already stranded in the world and their part in Hell forever.

What should our attitude be toward the Holy Spirit?

While the Holy Spirit is performing His assignment in us, we should:

- ✧ Obey His instructions at all times,
- ✧ Fellowship with Him on a daily basis,
- ✧ Ask Him for guidance,
- ✧ Allow His decisions to take precedence over ours,
- ✧ Pray in the Holy Spirit to get to God's presence and have God's favour,
- ✧ Live holy in thoughts, words and actions,
- ✧ Give Him all the glory for what He's doing in your life,
- ✧ Trust in Him only, and
- ✧ of course, study the word of God to know the best way to keep Him living in you.

Conclusion: Consistent disobedience may result in the departure of the Holy Spirit. When this occurs, the evil Spirit takes control, indicating that such a personality has been rejected, disowned, and dispossessed by God. He will be completely destroyed unless he repents (1 Samuel 15, 16:14, 31:1-end).

Questions

1. State 10 reasons why you need the Holy Spirit.
2. Quote Scripture references to support ways of receiving the Holy Spirit.

Notes

2nd QUARTERLY REVIEW

1. Mention at least five appropriate ways of worshipping God.
2. Explain "Mortification" according to lesson 14.
3. What is The Gate and Table of Show-Bread in appropriate worship?
4. Mention the items found in the Ark of Covenant and their meaning in worship.
5. Explain the Five circles of Christians briefly.
6. Give a brief description of known and unknown Christians to Christ and to the Disciples.
7. How can you distinguish Christianity from other world religions?

Printed in Great Britain
by Amazon